Resplendence of the
Spanish Monarchy

Monferrate

RESPLENDENCE

OF THE SPANISH MONARCHY

*Renaissance Tapestries and Armor from the
Patrimonio Nacional*

Antonio Domínguez Ortiz
Concha Herrero Carretero
José A. Godoy

THE METROPOLITAN MUSEUM OF ART, NEW YORK

DISTRIBUTED BY HARRY N. ABRAMS, INC., NEW YORK

This catalogue is published in conjunction with the exhibition
"Resplendence of the Spanish Monarchy: Renaissance Tapestries and Armor" held at
The Metropolitan Museum of Art, New York, October 11, 1991–January 5, 1992.

The exhibition has been organized with the cooperation of the Patrimonio Nacional of Spain.

The exhibition is made possible in part by the David H. Koch Charitable Foundation.

Transportation assistance has been provided by Iberia Airlines of Spain.

Published by The Metropolitan Museum of Art, New York

John P. O'Neill, Editor in Chief
M. E. D. Laing, Editor,
with the assistance of Rodolfo Aiello
Bruce Campbell, Designer
Susan Chun, Production

Photography by Bruce White,
The Photograph Studio, The Metropolitan Museum of Art

Other photograph credits: José A. Godoy, p. 108; Schecter Lee, p. 15; Museo Arqueológico Nacional,
Madrid, p. 19; Oronoz, S.A., Madrid, pp. 10, 13, 16 (Sánchez Coello), 17, 20, 22, 23
Map, p. 14, by Irmgard Lochner

Translated from the Spanish (texts by Antonio Domínguez Ortiz and Concha Herrero Carretero)
by Margaret Sayers Peden; and from the French (text by José A. Godoy) by Ellen van Haagen,
Ernst van Haagen, and Maurice Robine, Bertrand Languages Inc.

Composition by U.S. Lithograph, typographers, New York
Color separations by Professional Graphics, Rockford, Illinois
Printed by Julio Soto Impresor, S.A., Madrid
Bound by Encuadernación Ramos, S.A. Madrid

LIBRARY OF CONGRESS CATALOGING-IN-PUBLICATION DATA
Resplendence of the Spanish monarchy : Renaissance tapestries and armor
from the Patrimonio Nacional / Antonio Domínguez Ortiz, Concha Herrero Carretero, José A. Godoy.
p. cm. Catalogue of an exhibition. Includes bibliographical references.
ISBN 0-87099-621-5.—ISBN 0-8109-6408-2 (Abrams)
1. Tapestry, Renaissance—Spain—Exhibitions. 2. Tapestry—Spain—Exhibitions. 3. Armor,
Renaissance—Spain—Exhibitions. 4. Armor—Spain—Exhibitions. 5. Allegories—Exhibitions.
6. Art patronage—Spain—History—16th century—Exhibitions. I. Domínguez Ortiz, Antonio. II. Herrero Carretero, Concha.
III. Godoy, José A. IV. Patrimonio Nacional. V. Metropolitan Museum of Art (New York, N.Y.)
NK3062.AIR47 1991 739.7′0946′0747471—dc20 91-20158 CIP

FRONTISPIECE: *The Review of the Troops at Barcelona* (detail, cat. 9)
JACKET FRONT: Aurora, detail of *Atlas Supporting the Armillary Sphere* (cat. 6)
JACKET BACK: Parade shield of Charles V (cat. 23)

Contents

A Message from His Majesty King Juan Carlos I

The works of art that form the exhibition "Resplendence of the Spanish Monarchy: Renaissance Tapestries and Armor" have been under the care and protection of the Patrimonio Nacional for almost five centuries.

Many of these pieces were the special concern and delight of my predecessors Charles V and Philip II, who commissioned them, took a personal interest in their production, and rewarded the artists and craftsmen responsible. It is understandable, therefore, that with few exceptions these treasured objects have never left Spain.

Now, however, given the magnitude and distinction of the cultural initiative organized by the Patrimonio Nacional, an institution that almost from its inception has been closely bound to the Spanish Crown, and the importance of the celebrations marking the quincentennial of the discovery of America, commemorating as they do historic events of such profound and lasting significance, I am pleased to authorize the exhibition of these works collected by my forefathers. The tapestries and armor chosen cross the Atlantic for the first time, to be shown in the New World as a token of the friendship, good will, and close cultural ties that unite our peoples.

I salute the Patrimonio Nacional, encouraging it to persist in its cultural mission, and The Metropolitan Museum of Art in New York for offering itself as the setting for this event, which celebrates the cordial relations between the two institutions in the spirit of the quincentennial.

Foreword

The five-hundredth anniversary of the discovery of America in 1492 is an occasion to celebrate the meeting of the Old World and the New, and to renew the cultural dialogue between the two. It is in that spirit that the exhibition "Resplendence of the Spanish Monarchy: Renaissance Tapestries and Armor" has been conceived, motivating the Patrimonio Nacional of Spain to share with friends across the Atlantic some of the riches that it safeguards for the Spanish people. Drawn from two of the Patrimonio's most prized collections, these works offer a dazzling reflection of a period in Spain when regal magnificence depended in no small measure on the material resources of the New World.

The tapestries and armor presented here belonged—by inheritance, commission, or purchase—to two of Spain's most puissant monarchs: Charles I, who as Charles V ruled the Holy Roman Empire, and his son Philip II, a figure forever associated with the arts and with the monastery and palace of El Escorial. If we recall that Charles was born in 1500 and

Philip died in 1598, it is evident that the lives of father and son spanned almost the entire sixteenth century. Little wonder, then, that their collections afford a unique view of the cultural phenomenon we know as the Renaissance.

As patrons, the Spanish monarchs were in a position to call on the best that Europe could furnish. It is our great good fortune that in spite of the vicissitudes of time, so much that is superlative in the royal collections has survived. In turn, The Metropolitan Museum of Art in New York, repository of these works for a brief period, has its own outstanding collections of tapestries and armor, thereby enriching the cultural interaction. The Patrimonio Nacional of Spain welcomes the opportunity to offer the New World this glimpse of its holdings, as tribute to an event that for the history of Spain and the history of the world had such momentous, far-reaching consequences.

Manuel Gómez de Pablos
Presidente del Patrimonio Nacional

Foreword and Acknowledgments

The word *resplendence* carries with it implications of shining light and brilliant achievement. It is an especially apt term for an exhibition in which every single object is as noble in conception and execution as it is royal in provenance, each irradiating our view of the Renaissance. It was a signal honor when the Patrimonio Nacional of Spain approached us in 1988 with the idea of forming an exhibition of masterworks in its keeping. In the name of The Metropolitan Museum of Art, I wish to express to Their Majesties King Juan Carlos I and Queen Sofía and to the Patrimonio Nacional our profoundest gratitude for their willingness to share these works of art with an appreciative New World public.

Visitors privileged to stroll through the *reales sitios*, the royal buildings from which the objects in the exhibition are taken, come away with many vivid memories. Foremost might well be their recollections of the magnificent tapestries that line the interiors. Tapestries are present at every turn; indeed, they constitute the single most characteristic decorative element. A large stretch of the palace of San Ildefonso at Segovia is given over to a museum of tapestries. They enliven the walls of the Royal Palace in Madrid, those of El Escorial and Aranjuez, and even of Spanish embassies abroad. The Patrimonio Nacional has in its care more than one hundred and fifty from the sixteenth century alone, woven after cartoons by the grandest designers in the history of the art, including Bernaert van Orley and Giulio Romano. The eleven tapestries chosen here are among the most eloquent.

As for the Royal Armory, close by the Royal Palace in Madrid, it serves as an ideal introduction to Renaissance armor and weaponry. The visitor cannot fail to be enthralled by the compelling glamor of the pieces made for the Spanish monarchs—pieces fashioned of hard, flashing steel, yet given the most delicate embellishments imaginable. Again, the artists responsible

were the most sought after of their day. It is gratifying to be able to exhibit the Spanish royal armor at a time when the Metropolitan Museum's own Arms and Armor collection is being presented to the public in newly installed galleries, allowing abundant illuminating comparisons.

In planning an exhibition that would provide a reflection of Spain's Golden Age in the wake of her discovery of the New World, it seemed to us fitting to narrow its focus to the two areas of armor and tapestries, both evocative of Renaissance court life at its most splendid. Despite the difference of medium, they interrelate, resonating with a common language, effulgent alike with precious metal.

This exhibition is in every sense a collaborative effort of the Patrimonio Nacional and the Metropolitan Museum. Many dedicated people in both institutions have joined forces to bring the project to life, but there are two who, by their unflagging efforts, have been pivotal to its success. They are Manuel Gómez de Pablos, Presidente del Patrimonio Nacional, and Mahrukh Tarapor, Assistant Director at the Metropolitan Museum. Jonathan Brown, Carroll and Milton Petrie Professor at the Institute of Fine Arts, New York University, was instrumental at early stages of the exhibition's history, while Olga Raggio, Iris and B. Gerald Cantor Chairman of the department of European Sculpture and Decorative Arts at the Metropolitan Museum, played a prominent role in the selection of the objects.

In Spain, our thanks are due primarily to our colleagues Julio de la Guardia, Consejero Gerente del Patrimonio Nacional; Ramón Ledesma, Subdirector de Bienes Muebles Históricos y Museos del Patrimonio Nacional; Don Fernando Fernández Miranda, Jefe del Departamento de Conservación y Restauración del Patrimonio Nacional; Concha Herrero, Conservadora de la Colección de Tapices del Patrimonio Nacional; Pilar Benito, Conservadora de la Colección de Textiles del Patrimonio Nacional; Alvaro Soler, Conservador de la Real Armería del Palacio Real; and Fernanda Quintana, Jefe de Negociado de la Real Armería del Palacio Real. Javier Morales Vallejo and Fernando Martín proved to be invaluable guides to the collections. Plácido Arango, as always, has been a kind and helpful friend. Where the catalogue is concerned, we are grateful for the richly informed texts written by Antonio Domínguez Ortiz, member of the Real Academia de la Historia; by Concha Herrero; and by José A. Godoy, Conservateur des Armes et des Armures at the Musée d'Art et d'Histoire, Geneva, who has an unrivaled knowledge of the Royal Armory's holdings.

At the Metropolitan Museum, James David Draper, Curator, European Sculpture and Decorative Arts, served as coordinator of the exhibition and its catalogue. Stuart Pyhrr, Curator, Arms and Armor, and Alice Zrebiec, Associate Curator, European Sculpture and Decorative Arts, oversaw innumerable aspects of planning in their respective fields. Stuart Pyhrr contributed particularly generously to the prep-aration of the catalogue, which also benefited from the advice of Edith A. Standen, Consultant, European Sculpture and Decorative Arts. Produced by the Editorial Department under John P. O'Neill, Editor in Chief and General Manager of Publications, the catalogue reflects the expert attention of its editor, Mary Laing, and its designer, Bruce Campbell. Registrar John Buchanan and Assistant Secretary and Associate Counsel Sharon H. Cott addressed a multitude of details affecting the loan. The handsome installation of the galleries was planned by Michael Batista, Exhibition Designer. We are all indebted to Bruce White, Photographer, for extending the life of the exhibition through his glowing photography.

Factors of key importance have been the support of the David H. Koch Charitable Foundation, which has in part made the exhibition possible, and the transportation assistance provided by Iberia Airlines of Spain.

Philippe de Montebello
Director
The Metropolitan Museum of Art

Titian (ca. 1487/90–1576), *Charles V at the Battle of Mühlberg*, 1548. Madrid, Museo del Prado

Introduction: A Golden Age

Antonio Domínguez Ortiz

The collection of tapestries and armor presented in this volume belongs to a decisive epoch in the history of Spain and of the world, an epoch in which the last reflections of the Middle Ages were slowly fading in the dawn of the modern era—with no perceptible clash or difference between them. The two periods can be said to meet within a single integrating concept, that of the Renaissance, which was not merely an artistic and literary phenomenon but also an expression of every manifestation of human life. The Renaissance was a time of strongly contrasted light and shade, in which the most refined civilization existed side by side with evidence of an intolerance and brutality that we have no right to be shocked by, since we cannot be sure of having eradicated those elements from our own culture. It was an age of warfare, notable for great innovations in military science. At the same time it was profoundly concerned with religion and morality, preoccupied with Church reform and tarnished by acts of violence committed in the name of Christianity. It was an age of giants in the arena of intellectual accomplishment and of timeless aesthetic creations, an age of spiritual ferment stimulated by the recent invention of printing.

The Renaissance: Wealth and Patronage of the Arts

The Renaissance was also witness to the global expansion of Europe, facilitated by the enormous scientific and technical superiority it enjoyed with regard to other continents. And on the purely political level, the Renaissance was characterized by the strengthening of nation-states and the subordination of towns and feudal powers to absolute sovereigns who embodied the higher interests of the state. The inhabitants of the Iberian peninsula played a major role in these transformations. Not only were their lives changed at home, but an explosion of pent-up energies also carried them over and far beyond their borders. Situated within the confines of Europe, the Iberian peoples found themselves, as a consequence of the great voyages of discovery, in a privileged geostrategic position: at the confluence of maritime routes linking Europe, Africa, and America.

Because of their active participation in those discoveries, the Spanish and Portuguese were at the center of the political stage, and their accumulated wealth gave them ready access to the treasures of the Renaissance. There was a busy trade in imports from Italy and Flanders, the two great centers of the Renaissance, and a multitude of artists traveled to the Iberian peninsula to satisfy the demands both of the Church and of the princes and great lords whose incomes allowed them to satisfy their every want and to indulge their patronage of the arts.

The grand design of the Catholic Kings, Isabella of Castile (1451–1504) and Ferdinand of Aragon (1452–1516), was to unite the five kingdoms of the peninsula into a single entity. Their first task was to eliminate the Islamic kingdom of Granada, a goal they achieved in 1492 following ten years of bloody struggle. The armies that later fought in Italy were forged in that crucible, and the crusading spirit—half-missionary, half-martial—that fueled the struggle against Islam found its sequel in the adventure of the New World.

The union between the kingdoms of Castile and Aragon, with the later addition of Navarre, was formed on the basis of equality: the predominance of Castile was determined by its greater land mass and larger population, not by its institutional superiority. The kingdoms associated under the rule of one royal house maintained their own laws, coinage, emblems, and town councils. The desire of Ferdinand and Isabella to join the kingdom of Portugal to this federation, which manifested itself in a series of royal alliances, was thwarted for a time by biological accidents but later allowed Philip II, who was as much Portuguese as Castilian, to rule over the entire peninsula. There was also intense cultural communication between the two peoples: Castilian professors taught at the University of Coimbra, and many Portuguese students attended the University of Salamanca. Several of the best-known Portuguese authors of the period habitually wrote in Spanish.

The year 1492 was the most decisive in the history of Spain: Ferdinand and Isabella made a triumphant entry into the Alhambra of Granada, the fortress-palace of the last monarchs of the Nasrid dynasty; the eminent humanist Antonio de Nebrija published the first Spanish grammar; and on October 12, Christopher Columbus, commanding three ships crewed by a hundred men, reached landfall in the Americas. Another event of a very different nature occurred that year: an order was given that caused a hundred thousand Jews to be expelled from Spain, a decree that brought a thousand years of coexistence to an abrupt halt. Some Jews remained in Spain, integrated into Christian society or exposed to the rigors of the Inquisition. Despite the cultural impoverishment that was unquestionably the result of that act, the sixteenth century still deserves to be called the *Siglo de Oro*, the Golden Age of Spain.

The cultural splendor of the age was due to a favorable economic situation, stimulated by the gold and silver from the Indies and by the multiple contacts that resulted from a foreign policy of active engagement, very much directed toward other countries in Europe. Once the great consolidation of power we have referred to was effected, Ferdinand and Isabella expanded their area of influence in many different directions, sometimes calling on diplomacy, at which they were masters, sometimes relying on commercial relations, and sometimes (*ultima ratio regum*) employing the force of arms. One area of expansion was North Africa, an undertaking thought of as a continuation of the Reconquest, the Crusade against Islam. Later, although North Africa never disappeared from the Spanish rulers' horizon, problems in Europe and the much stronger attraction of the American enterprise caused the Maghreb to take second place in their order of priorities. The strongholds they maintained there (Ceuta, Melilla, Oran), like islands in a hostile sea, were regarded not so much as bases from which to penetrate the interior as defensive outposts, inadequate though they were, against the pirates constantly threatening the coasts of the Iberian peninsula.

Italy, the Low Countries, and Spain

Expansion in Italy derived from the continuing interest of the crown of Aragon in the southern part of the Italian peninsula and the islands of Sicily and Sardinia. In the kingdom of Naples, the Catalan-Aragon dynasty was threatened by the ambitions of the French. After the end of the Hundred Years' War, France viewed Italy as a country filled with natural and human riches but one also made an easy prey by the inherent weakness of its political divisions. For the Spanish rulers, Italy had a second focus of attraction: the Holy Apostolic See, which, in addition to embodying supreme spiritual authority, had constructed in the heart of Italy a state to be contended with in the political alignments played out on a complex chessboard. The force of arms favored Ferdinand and Isabella: after a cruel struggle the French were driven from Italy. Later, during the time of Charles V, the duchy of Milan—which, besides being a very fertile region, commanded the Alpine passes—was added to the Spanish domain. A number of small Italian states, while not directly controlled, remained under Spanish influence. Only two states—Venice in the northeast and Savoy in the northwest—retained a stubborn independence.

Fortune also smiled on Ferdinand in the area of papal power. In that same decisive year of 1492 a Spaniard, a Valencian named Rodrigo de Borja—or Borgia, as he was known in Italy—was elected pope. Rodrigo took the name Alexander VI; he followed a policy of accommodation, and in exchange for favors for himself and his followers he granted the king and queen of Spain everything they desired. He bestowed upon each of them the title of Catholic King, and promulgated the famous bulls that divided lands and oceans yet to be discovered between the Spanish and Portuguese. He also reserved for Ferdinand and Isabella the prerogative of conquering North Africa, a questionable privilege that they never used. Nor did they claim, other than in the long list of royal titles,

The Catholic Kings: Ferdinand II of Aragon and Isabella I of Castile (details of *The Virgin and Child with the Catholic Kings*, artist unknown, ca. 1490). Madrid, Museo del Prado

the names "King and Queen of Jerusalem," which the bellicose Pope Julius II accorded them in the hope of fanning their crusading zeal. Relations with the Holy See were not always amicable, however, and at times were very stormy. There was, for example, open warfare between Charles V and Clement VII, with the Sack of Rome in 1527 as its deplorable result, and between Philip II and Paul IV hostilities were renewed. Yet, on the whole, owing to a combination of political and religious interests, the papacy was one of the strongest supporters of the Spanish cause.

A different area of expansion and of reciprocal influence was represented by the Low Countries—the region that today consists of the Benelux economic union, together with a sizable portion of northeastern France. If Italy was the great hub of the Renaissance in the south, in the north another, more austere Renaissance radiated its own light, seeking in the ideals of pagan and Christian antiquity inspiration and models for a renewal of the arts, religious fervor, and mores. The birthplace of superb painters, of human-

ists of the stature of Erasmus of Rotterdam, those lands were a hive of industry, whose people expressed their enjoyment of life in boisterous festivals and at the same time exported products that often transcended the artisanal level to become works of art. This was true of the manufacture of tapestries, in which the country that is today Belgium, and specifically the city of Brussels, displayed unquestionable superiority.

Economic relations between Castile and Flanders intensified toward the end of the Middle Ages; this interchange was based on export of the incomparable merino wool, the heritage, it would seem, of Islam and the exclusive patrimony of Castile. The center of the Spanish wool trade was Burgos, which in the final years of the Middle Ages was completing, with the notable assistance of German artists, its magnificent Gothic cathedral. From Burgos, after crossing the mountains, wool was shipped from Bilbao and Laredo, destined for English, French, and above all Flemish ports: Antwerp, Rotterdam, Ostend. There was a Spanish mercantile consulate in Bruges until the end of the seventeenth century. In exchange for wool, olive oil, and other agricultural products, ships on their return voyage carried textiles of superior quality, arms and armor, and a multitude of luxury items: books, watches, paintings, expensive furniture, tapestries, and jewels. The consignees of these imported goods were aristocrats, members of the higher clergy, and wealthy citizens eager to embellish their homes. The Spanish royal house was a loyal customer for Flemish merchandise, a fact demonstrated, for example, by the collection of Flemish paintings acquired by Isabella the Catholic and displayed today in the Capilla Real in Granada. When the Netherlands became part of the Spanish kingdom, the relationship grew even stronger, and during the sixteenth and seventeenth centuries, the tapestry workshops of Brussels and Oudenaarde filled many commissions from the Spanish court.

One aspect of relations between Spain and Flanders was profoundly spiritual, with interesting consequences. The influence of Erasmus was nowhere more intense than in Spain, where copies of his works sold by tens of thousands, to the point of alarming the more conservative sectors of the Church. A disciple and companion of Erasmus was the Spaniard Juan Luis Vives, a humanist who fled his native Valencia out of fear of the Inquisition, which had destroyed his family, Jewish in origin. Many other Spaniards had intellectual connections with Flanders. A notable example is Benito Arias Montano, who collaborated in the major enterprise of editing and printing the Polyglot Bible of Antwerp.

It is not easy to explain in a few words how the

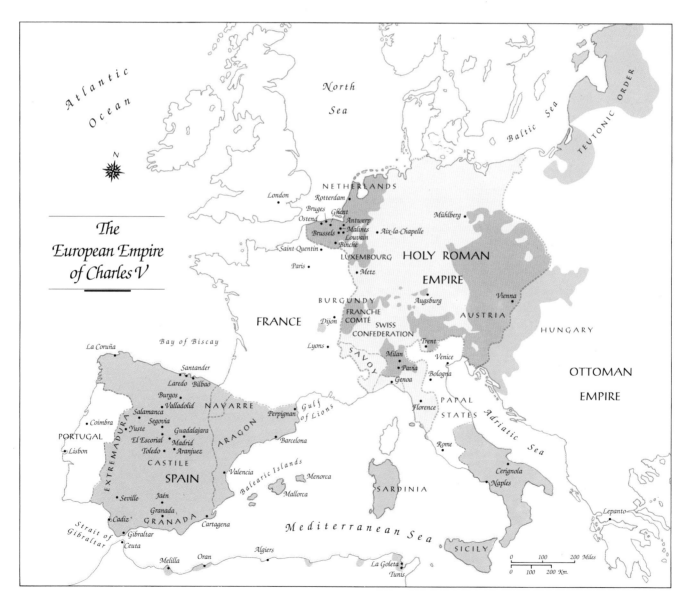

The European Empire of Charles V

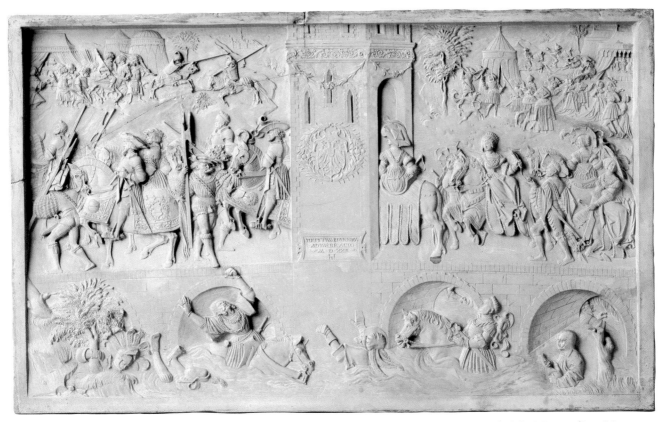

Hans Daucher (ca. 1485–1539), *Allegory of Virtues and Vices at the Court of Charles V*, 1522. New York, The Metropolitan Museum of Art, Gift of J. Pierpont Morgan, 1917. The young emperor is the horseman in the foreground on the left; emerging from the arch behind him is Frederick II, Count Palatine. The Turkish encampment above is a reminder of the threat presented by the Ottoman Empire.

Low Countries came to be incorporated into the enormous political complex governed by Charles V, which then was called the Spanish, or Hapsburg, monarchy. Its beginnings go back to the High Middle Ages, when there was an attempt to create a state from the union of Germany and France, stretching from the Rhine to the Meuse. After repeated failures, the dukes of Burgundy seemed close to realizing this ideal in the fourteenth century. Their domains extended from Friesland to the border of Switzerland. Their court was one of the most lavish, their Order of the Golden Fleece one of the most sought after, and although within the feudal system the dukes were vassals of the kings of France, they acted with complete autonomy.

The violent death of Charles the Bold, duke of Burgundy, in 1477, placed that imposing edifice in danger of collapse. King Louis XI of France annexed Burgundy and made no secret of his intentions with regard to the remaining territories. To counter this threat, Mary, the only heir of Charles the Bold, was married to the German emperor Maximilian, a Haps-burg and head of the house of Austria. Two children born of this union were destined to marry heirs to the Spanish crown: the marriage of Margaret of Burgundy with the firstborn of Ferdinand and Isabella had no political consequences because of her husband's early death; but from the marriage between Philip the Handsome (1478–1506) and Juana of Castile (1479–1555) —Juana la Loca, or Joanna the Mad—would be born Charles I of Spain, the man who as Emperor Charles V best symbolized the idea of the unity of Europe and the one who with the greatest bitterness watched over the failure of that idea.

Charles V (1500–1558): The Spanish Monarchy

Charles was born in Ghent in 1500, in an atmosphere of jubilation and hope. The conquest of Granada had eliminated the Islamic threat to western Europe. Although Islam was still very strong to the east, it directly threatened only populations separated physically by distance and spiritually by the religious

Leone Leoni (1509–1590), Cameo of Charles V and his son Philip II (obverse), and Isabella of Portugal, Charles's wife and Philip's mother (reverse), 1550. New York, The Metropolitan Museum of Art, The Milton Weil Collection, Gift of Ethel S. Worgelt, 1938

schism that attempts at reconciliation had been unable to heal. More good news had come from the west: the discovery of islands that because of their size, their vegetation, and the racial characteristics of their inhabitants—different from any known before—presaged the existence of a New World. Under the dual protection of the Hapsburgs and the kings of Spain, the states that formed the Burgundian legacy could enjoy in peace the advantages afforded by their privileged location—at the crossroads between countries of advanced and long-established civilization, traversed by navigable rivers, and studded with presti-

gious cities in which cathedrals and monasteries rose beside splendid town halls and merchants' guildhalls. Then as now, those territories were divided into two major linguistic areas—French-speaking and Dutch-speaking—although the distinction was less important than it is today. There was a cultural unity symbolized by the use of Latin in the sciences; there was a religious unity that was destined to be sundered; and there was a political unity based on adherence to a sovereign who in turn assured ample autonomy to each of the regions.

This cosmopolitan ambience was reinforced in the case of Charles V by the mixture of blood that flowed in his veins and by the many contacts forced on him by the obligations of empire. Francophone by birth, he was later, of necessity, polyglot. The untimely death of his father and his mother's incapacity saddled him early with the burdens of office. Traveling incessantly, he bore the weight of innumerable worries and great responsibilities, all of which contributed in no small measure to his premature old age.

The inheritance that fell to the young Charles following the deaths of his parents and grandparents cannot be defined in juridical or political terms. It was not an empire, because there was no mother

RIGHT: Alonso Sánchez Coello (1531/32–1588), *The Daughters of Philip II*, ca. 1571. Madrid, Monasterio de las Descalzas Reales. Behind the princesses, Isabella Clara Eugenia (on the right) and Catalina Micaela, is a view of the royal residence in Madrid, the Alcázar de las Austrias, destroyed by fire in 1734; the present Royal Palace was erected on the same site, 1738–64.

OPPOSITE: Artist unknown, *View of the Monastery-Palace of San Lorenzo del Escorial*, 17th century. El Escorial. Completed in 1584, the Escorial was built by Philip II to commemorate the Spanish victory over the French at Saint-Quentin on the feast of St. Lawrence (August 10), 1557. The architects were Juan Bautista de Toledo and after his death, Juan de Herrera.

country with subordinate territories. It was not a multination state, because the proper organs of state were lacking. There was no common tongue, no capital, no body of laws, no coinage in general use. The single bond among the different kingdoms, principalities, duchies, and seigniories was the person of the sovereign, who exacted from each territory the funds necessary to run the body politic while respecting individual usages and customs. This very lack of political definition facilitated coexistence. The countries of Europe would never have accepted a regime that gave the appearance of uniformity or centralization. The title of Emperor bestowed on Charles in 1519 by the Imperial Diet was more an idea or symbol than a sign of effective power. The Hapsburgs wielded true power in the patrimonial states of Austria; in Germany the degree of obeisance accorded by secular and ecclesiastical princes and free cities depended on their own strength and the emperor's diplomatic skill. Hence the infinite patience displayed by Charles V when religious disputes divided the German empire; he knew that resorting to force, even if it resulted in initial success, would end badly, and experience proved him right.

The price of that immense power was the need to confront a host of enemies both at home and abroad, a constant tension that ended by wrecking his nerves and causing him—even before his abdication—to long for seclusion, solitude, and tranquillity of spirit. But such a state of mind could not be allowed to prevail; the successor to the Roman Caesars, crowned in Bologna in 1530 by Pope Clement VII in a resplendent ceremony, could show no overt signs of weakness. If all princely life is a perpetual performance, it must have been excessively so for Charles: praised by poets, anointed by the Church, acclaimed by the masses. To be seen as a symbol rather than a man is undoubtedly a heavy burden to bear.

The Renaissance Court

Charles V fulfilled his responsibilities with great dignity and played the game according to the rules. He posed for Titian; he acted as patron to Aretino, whose pen was more dangerous than a hundred swords. Propaganda was both the task of imperial chroniclers and a court art. At this time, as we have pointed out, no central capital existed; in his incessant travels Charles V was housed in palaces, *alcázares*, and monasteries. During his sojourns in

Spain, he stayed for long periods in the Alcázar of Toledo. He began his honeymoon with Isabella of Portugal in the Alcázar of Seville and continued it during his long stay in the Alhambra in Granada, when he sought to resolve the complicated problems arising from the conquest of the Muslim kingdom. He also resided in Madrid and in Valladolid, the city in which the child destined to be his successor was born. In each of these places, where he was surrounded by a circle of intimates and by his guard, the royal chamberlain tried to create an ambience worthy of a princely residence. There was, however, no true court, nor could there be. A court was incompatible with such a peripatetic existence.

In the Low Countries there was both a capital and a court: Brussels. It was Brussels that in 1555 witnessed the moving ceremony of Charles's abdication, and from then on it was the residence of the regents of the Netherlands. The pomp and ceremony and etiquette that had surrounded the dukes of Burgundy were transplanted to the court of Spain; the setting was the Alcázar of Madrid, where Philip II fixed his capital in 1561. Philip was not a king given to luxury, however, and he spent much of his time in the more austere Escorial. It was not until the reign of his son Philip III that the opulent life of the Spanish Hapsburgs began to unfold in all its imposing flamboyance—along with the astronomical expenditures repeatedly denounced by the Castilian Cortes, amid pleas to the sovereign to curtail his extravagance and restore the activities of his house to the simplicity that had characterized it under Ferdinand and Isabella.

Complaints about excessive expenditures are easily understood. In taking over the Burgundian household, the Spanish monarchy continued to maintain the staff of the house of Castile, producing, in many instances, a duplication of functions. There were physicians attached to the house of Burgundy, for example, and physicians for the house of Castile. Because of this dual history, positions at the Spanish court with Spanish titles coexisted with similar posts whose French names indicated their Burgundian origins; a case in point was the *mayordomo mayor*, or chief steward, with his counterpart the *summiler* [*sommelier*] *de corps*. Altogether, the royal palace housed thousands

of individuals, not counting courtiers, visitors, and the whole complex world that whirled around that center of power. The court was a self-sufficient city, with daily deliveries of the enormous quantities of foodstuffs, firewood, and goods needed to maintain the well-being of the people and animals that lived there (hundreds of horses occupied the stables). And there were secondary residences where royalty took up temporary quarters, depending on the season of the year. In the seventeenth century the expenses of the court came to consume ten percent of the state's income.

For the monarchs, the negative side of existence in a sumptuous and refined setting graced with innumerable works of art was finding themselves subject to a ceremonial system that turned every act of their lives into a minutely regulated ritual. The royal passion for hunting is explained in large part by a desire to escape the stifling ceremony imposed by Charles V in 1545 and codified as the "Etiquetas de la Casa de Austria" (Protocol of the House of Austria). This code of conduct was undoubtedly the strictest of all those prevailing in the European courts, and it survived in the imperial court of Vienna long after its attrition or total disappearance in Spain. The contrast with the court of France was striking, for there the royal palace was open to all the nobles, and they in turn contributed to making its life more brilliant and animated. The construction in the seventeenth century of the Buen Retiro Palace in Madrid, whose gracious buildings set amid extensive gardens were very different from the massive ensemble of the Alcázar, helped improve the situation, but until the end the Hapsburg court continued to be a dignified, solemn, and somewhat stultifying place, in which the sovereign lived a rather isolated life with few opportunities to relate to his subjects.

Court Art, Religion, and Mythology in the Tapestries

Although each nation had its own style, the court art of Europe shared certain similarities and general characteristics. At a time when great lords enjoyed huge incomes and magnificent residences, it was indispensable for the sovereign to surpass them in the luxury of his palaces, the ostentation of his ceremonies, and the number of his servants. Therein lies the secret of expenditures that today strike us as outrageous. The possession of jewels, enormous quantities of silverware, armor, religious relics, precious manuscripts, paintings, carpets, and tapestries also formed part of the *vida noble*, the noble life, and in this, too, royalty had to outdo any of its vassals. By good fortune, Spanish monarchs were connoisseurs and lovers of art in all its manifestations. Their domains embraced a great many territories, several of them deservedly famous for artistic creation. The two great centers of the Renaissance, Italy and Flanders, were under their influence or direct control. The Spanish rulers received extremely valuable gifts and in addition spent large sums in purchases and commissions. Numerous artists worked exclusively for the court. Because of all these factors, the quantity of precious objects accumulated in the royal palaces was so great that, even after the losses sustained over the years, we are still astounded by their number and quality.

In general terms, court art fits within the secular and profane current that runs through the Renaissance as a continuation of the chivalric culture of the Middle Ages, distinct from but not antithetical to the predominantly religious vein of the time. Court art did not exclude sacred subjects, but it made much use of historical and mythological themes and tended to heroize the sovereigns, imputing to them every virtue and matching them with the great figures and myths of classical antiquity. Within the Christian tradition, the king was the representative of God; to attack him was sacrilege. In terms of chivalry, on the other hand, he was seen above all as a military commander defending his people.

The two currents met in the person of Charles V. Placed as he was between the Middle Ages and the modern world, he symbolized both the paladin waging war against the infidel and the prototype of the Christian knight defined by Erasmus: religious without being superstitious, guardian of the law, protector of the weak and oppressed. Artists and poets made of the king an icon laden with all the rhetoric, all the symbols of Greco-Roman tradition. The comparison with Mars was obvious, for he was a "thunderbolt of war." This was not a king to direct military operations from his study; in Tunis, in Mühlberg, in Metz, he shared the hardships of the campaign with his soldiers. Titian had good cause, therefore, to paint him on a galloping steed, his lance at the ready. Nor is it strange that poets compared him to the god of war, praising him even as the greater:

> Had there been two of Mars, he would be the first,
> And Mars the second of the two.

But the mythological fiction was cold and unreal. No one could seriously believe that the emperor was a second Mars. A comparison with Hercules, by contrast, was much more convincing; he, too, was a symbol of strength and power, and as the son of a mortal he was closer to men than to the gods. The figure of Hercules was remarkably popular in the sixteenth century. The hero and his legendary Labors were represented everywhere: in frontispieces, triumphal arches, paintings, tapestries, armor, books. Reading the chroniclers of the time, one has the impression that they thought of Hercules as a real person. The founding of Seville was attributed to him, and the construction of its walls; likewise the founding of La Coruña and the building of its famous tower (in truth, a Roman lighthouse), as well as the tower of Cadiz, near the site of the famous temple in which Hercules was worshiped and of the legendary pillars that marked the limits of the known world. Undoubtedly, Charles and those around him shared these notions, for at a very early date, 1516, in keeping with the custom of selecting a personal motto and device, he chose for himself that of *Plus Ultra*. It was a good choice, because in physical terms his empire extended far beyond the Strait of Gibraltar, and in an allegorical sense it indicated his will to surpass, to be universal. No device has ever had such success: stamped on Spanish silver coins it made its way around the world,

Double scudo of Charles V, from the mint of Milan under the direction of Leone Leoni, ca. 1550. Madrid, Museo Arqueológico Nacional

and the dollar sign—the stylized pillars of the two vertical bars and the curves of the pennon that contained the motto—is to this day a living witness to the myth.

The apogee of the allegorical exaltation of the prince corresponds to the first half of the sixteenth century; artists and writers collaborated in this enterprise—we have only to think of Leone Leoni's magnificent sculpture *Charles V Defeating Heresy*. The Spanish court was characterized by a more devout atmosphere than other European courts, a feature that is evident in repeated series of tapestries on religious themes. There are also a few curious examples that, very much in the spirit of the age, combine the religious with the profane: thus, in the set of tapestries known as *Los Honores*, Fame and Fortune appear together with representations of Faith, Justice, and other Christian virtues.

The tendency toward purely Christian subject matter, or toward the interpretation of pagan themes in Christian terms, grew stronger as the sixteenth century progressed and as the mentality in Europe changed, with ideas of harmony and reform giving way to more hostile feelings that found an outlet in religious persecutions and civil wars. Charles V experienced this change as both personal and political tragedy. The conciliatory nature he had shown in 1526 during his stay in Granada, when he accorded the newly converted Moriscos a grace period of forty years in which they might retain their language, dress, and customs, had also impelled him to seek a peaceful solution to the disputes between Protestants and Catholics by convoking a general council which representatives of both sides were to attend. The Protestants did not participate, however, believing that they lacked sufficient guarantees, and the Council of Trent stamped its seal on the division. Europe split into three zones: one in the north, where Protestantism had an easy triumph; another in the south, where Catholicism asserted itself; and a broad area reaching from France to Hungary, in which long years of bitter warfare perpetuated and reinforced the division between the two faiths.

It was not in the emperor's character to tolerate disharmony. Protestant resistance insulted his faith as a Catholic and his authority as a monarch. In his last years little remained of his early conciliatory temperament, and from his monastic retreat at Yuste he exhorted his son Philip to be severe in his repression of the signs of Lutheranism that were springing up throughout Spain. Charles did not live to see the tragedy of Flanders, although the first sparks of the future conflagration flared during the last years of his reign. None could doubt his great affection for the Low Countries. It was not from any spirit of local patriotism, however. When Ghent revolted, he dealt with the city harshly, regardless of the fact that it was his birthplace. What he cared about was the whole of Charles the Bold's legacy, prompted by a sense of family solidarity, an identification with the dynasty, a lineage so vigorous then, so attenuated today. Despite his slow Hispanicization, Charles's memoirs were written in the French of his childhood. He never

Leone Leoni (1509–1590), *Charles V Defeating Heresy*, 1551–53. Madrid, Museo del Prado

quite saw the modern state in terms of the impersonal and the abstract, and it was this that contributed to his supranational vision of Europe. In his concept (characteristically medieval), the bond that united his dynasty with its peoples was the vassal–lord relationship, based on loyalty to individuals, to an actual family. Hence his determination to recover Burgundy, the cradle of his ancestors. In this he was unsuccessful; Francis I had annexed Burgundy to France, invoking specifically nationalistic motives. Nevertheless, as a permanent vindication of their claim, Charles V and his successors continued to describe as Burgundian the Franche Comté, Luxembourg, and the whole of the Low Countries. In 1548 these territories were finally admitted into the empire under the collective name of Burgundy, although, as Henri Pirenne notes, it was a purely formal incorporation, the only effect of which was the collection of a few taxes for defense against the Turks.

Philip II (1527–1598): The New Art of War

Charles, who had directed the conquest of Tunis in 1535 with such lofty ambitions, later accepted defeat in Algiers and showed no reaction to the loss of Tripoli. In his will there is not a single word devoted to the African territories. This omission indicates the extent to which in his later years his attention was concentrated on Europe. In his judgment, the greatest danger threatening Europe was internal, not external, and his son, Philip II, was of the same opinion. Although less attached to Flanders than his father, he did not hesitate to start a politico-religious war that was to last eighty years. There were several reasons for this undertaking. First, Philip II, his son, and his grandson all considered themselves Burgundian; it was a family matter. Second, at stake was an extremely valuable part of their empire. Third, they felt obliged to defend the Catholic faith. The three motivations combined in different proportions that varied over time, with a tendency toward greater politicization of the conflict at the expense of its religious aspects.

After Philip II's stay in Flanders during his youth, no Spanish sovereign ever again visited the Burgundian territories. All the more moving, therefore, is the unswerving loyalty of his vassals, especially those in the Franche Comté who, surrounded on all sides by the French, defended their land with no outside help. It would be excessive to say that they acted out of loyalty to Spain; more realistically, they felt bound to the distant prince who guaranteed them broad domestic autonomy. For them, belonging to the Spanish crown did not mean being Spanish but, rather, having the assurance that they would never be absorbed by France. In the Low Countries, things were more complicated: the Catholics, dominant in the south in what today is Belgium, found Spanish support against the Calvinists of the north, today's Holland; both were very unhappy, however, about encroachments on their secular liberties and privileges. At the end of his reign, weary of the long war and its intolerable expense, Philip II decided to relinquish his grasp on the Netherlands, ceding them to his daughter Isabella and his son-in-law Archduke Albert of Austria, on condition that in exchange for their vassalage and his corresponding obligation to defend them, the status quo should remain virtually unchanged. As the marriage produced no heirs, Flanders reverted to the Spanish crown, continuing to act as a barrier against French expansionism and to supply Spain with the products of its industry. From Flemish presses came a host of books by Spanish authors, while Flemish paintings, tapestries, and other works of art continued to embellish both royal palaces (Madrid, El Escorial, Aranjuez, El Pardo) and seignorial mansions.

Philip II was the last of the Spanish Hapsburgs to be present on the field of battle, at Saint-Quentin in 1557. From then on comparisons with Mars or Hercules were no longer appropriate; the rupture with the ways of Charles V was complete. There is an evident parallelism in this with the social evolution of Spain. In the reign of the Catholic Kings, Spanish society was a martial one, with an appetite and a vocation for the military. The art of warfare was not a closed profession but a normal stage in a man's life, especially in that of a hidalgo, or minor noble; nearly all had arms in their houses, and the higher ranks of the nobility possessed real arsenals. Despite almost total peace at home, there were still noblemen engaged in building fortified castles—for example, the

Anthonis Mor (ca. 1516/19–1576),
Portrait of Philip II, ca. 1557.
El Escorial

Juan de Orea, *The Battle of Pavia*, 1550–63. Granada, Alhambra, Palace of Charles V

castle of Canena, near Jaén, constructed by Don Francisco de los Cobos, secretary to the emperor.

The sixteenth century witnessed two waves of change: on the technical side, the definitive triumph of firearms over edged weapons, and on the social, a growing disinclination to serve in the military, which offered fewer and fewer opportunities for personal enrichment. By the end of the century, the Spanish nobility was showing signs of indolence, of becoming almost bourgeois in its values. The number of young volunteers willing to carry a pike for the king in Flanders was steadily decreasing. In the seventeenth century this decline assumed such proportions that the count-duke of Olivares attempted to reverse the trend, seeing in the loss of a military vocation among the Spanish nobility one of the most direct causes of his country's decadence.

Armor and Social Symbols

A series of symbols had already been created, however, that depended upon the warlike nature of the king and his nobles, and these symbols tended to endure even though the original reasons for their existence had disappeared. Lances, swords, and armor continued to play a symbolic role long after kings and nobles had ceased to use them. The surrender of the sword was a rite that signified the defeat of a rival. Boabdil's sword, for example, was the trophy that visibly recalled, even to the uneducated, the conquest of Granada by Ferdinand and Isabella. The sword of Francis I, taken prisoner at Pavia in 1525, was kept in Madrid until it was returned to France by order of Napoleon.

The quality of offensive and defensive arms corresponded, naturally, to the economic status of their owners. *Caballeros* (knights) were so named because they could stable a horse (*caballo*) and maintain the necessary servants. By the end of the Middle Ages armor had acquired an extraordinary beauty and perfection—at a price, too, that exaggerated the distinction between noblemen and those who could afford only a buckler to defend themselves. In the south of

Spain there was an intermediate category, the *caballeros de cuantía*, analogous to the *caballeros villanos* of Castile. Both groups were composed of wealthy commoners who, because they could afford a horse and weapons, enjoyed some of the privileges of rank.

These intermediate classes disappeared when the conquest of Granada and the peace established inside Spain rendered their services superfluous. In France the civil wars of the second half of the sixteenth century kept alive the fighting spirit of the nobility in that country at the very moment it was declining in Spain. Together with these psychological transformations, other changes—this time of a technical order—helped to relegate armor to the status of the purely ornamental. True works of art for decorative purposes only, fine armor continued to be made for the kings of Spain. Kings and princes continued to be represented in martial attitudes in paintings and equestrian sculptures. The similarity between the scepter, symbol of sovereignty, and the baton, emblem of military power, facilitated the fusion of the two roles. Nobiliary ideology continued to permeate society, and the idea of nobility was inseparable from the martial arts as consecrated by tradition. The invention of firearms was accepted only much later and with many reservations. In theory, royalty could appear on the battlefield with lance, sword, or baton, but never carrying a musket or harquebus. Noble arms still meant edged weapons. The Spanish kings' love of the hunt was what saved them from this contretemps, allowing a firearm to be placed in their

Workshop of Pompeo Leoni (ca. 1533–1608), *Bust of Philip II*, ca. 1575. New York, The Metropolitan Museum of Art, Bequest of Annie C. Kane, 1926

hands without loss of dignity, offering a new theme to artists and humanizing the person of the king, converting majestic symbols into everyday reality. Never again would the exaltation of martial deeds and skills by means of art reach such heights as in this Golden Age.

Renaissance Tapestries from the Patrimonio Nacional

CONCHA HERRERO CARRETERO

FORTVNA

Los Honores

 The set of tapestries known as *Los Honores*—literally, *The Honors*—was woven by Pieter van Aelst, famous tapestry maker to the court of Brussels, and was listed in early inventories of the Oficio de Tapicería, the Tapestry Office, under the name "Fortune." The events that motivated its fabrication were the election in 1519 of Charles of Hapsburg, since 1516 King Charles I of Spain, as Holy Roman Emperor, and his coronation in Aix-la-Chapelle on October 23, 1520, a date woven into the *Fortune* tapestry.

The nine hangings that make up the set were completed in 1523. Because of financial difficulties, however, Pieter van Aelst found himself in the position of having to mortgage the set to the Antwerp agents of the Fuggers, a German family of merchant princes. Van Aelst suggested to his creditors that they first offer the costly tapestries for sale to His Imperial Majesty Charles V, the person in whose honor they had been woven. The suggestion was accepted, and as a sample the central piece of the set, representing an allegory of Honor, was sent to the emperor. He did not come into possession of the remaining tapestries until 1526, when in Seville, the city where he and Isabella of Portugal were married.

An iconographic analysis of *Los Honores* demonstrates that the set reflects an allegorical and moralistic scheme related to sixteenth-century principles of royal ethics. The individual tapestries were meant to instruct the young sovereign in virtues to be practiced and vices to be shunned, with the aim of obtaining the highest of all rewards: Honor, Fame (Good Repute), and Nobility.

Literary allusions abound, especially to the writings of Alain de Lille and Jean Lemaire de Belges, along with the standard works of Ovid, Valerius Maximus, Boccaccio, and Petrarch.

Numerous as they must have been, there is no documentary evidence to identify the painters who executed the cartoons for the tapestries, nor has any preparatory sketch survived. The designs were unquestionably the work of several artists, chief among them Bernaert van Orley and Jan Gossart called Mabuse.

The iconographic order established by Professor Guy Delmarcel of the University of Louvain aligns the tapestries in two groups of four on either side of the one representing Honor (stairways shown in the tapestries *Faith* and *Fame*, on the right and left respectively, are part of the steps leading to the tribunal over which Honor presides): *Fortune; Prudence; Divine Truth; Faith; Honor; Fame; Justice; Nobility; Infamy.*[1]

1. Delmarcel 1971.

OPPOSITE: Blind Fortune, "strewing roses on this side, tossing stones on that" (detail of cat. 1, upper center)

27

I *Fortune*

Los Honores: first tapestry
Workshop of Pieter van Aelst (active 1495–1531), after a
cartoon attributed to Bernaert van Orley (ca. 1491–1541/42)
Brussels, 1520–23
Dated: 1520
Gold, silver, silk, and wool
16 ft. 1 in. x 28 ft. 2 in. (490 x 860 cm.)
Segovia, Museo de Tapices, Palacio de San Ildefonso
Inv. PN. S.8/5

The goddess Fortune, eyes blindfolded, rides across
the heavens on a charger, scattering roses with her
right hand upon those she favors and stones with her
left upon her victims. Below her is the wheel of Fortune, governed by a woman, floating between two
seas. Arrayed on the upper rim of the wheel are the
attributes of empire: crown, scepter, and sword. The
fortunate, presided over by Phoebus Apollo at the
upper left, occupy one side of this central axis, the
unfortunate, showered by bolts from Vulcan's forge,
the other. Derived from mythology, ancient history,
and the Bible, and exemplifying the main theme,
the different characters can be identified not only by
their attributes but also by the names woven into the
tapestry.[2]

The upper edge of the border of flowers and fruit
on a dark background incorporates three scrolls bearing Latin inscriptions that comment on the scenes immediately below them:

> *Omnia vel voto longe meliora feruntur*
> *Ipsaq[ue] Mors presens, Sorte fauente, fugit.*

> (All things are better borne through hope, and death
>   itself,
> Though imminent, flees when the lot is favorable.)

> *Hinc spargens fortuna rosas hi[n]c saxa voluta[n]s*
> *Ludit et arbitrio cu[n]cta suopte regit.*

> (Fortune, strewing roses on this side, tossing stones on
>   that,
> Makes merry and guides all things by her whim.)

> *Nil nisi triste cadit, quibus est fortuna sinistra*
> *Milleq[ue] funestis Mors venit atra modis.*

> (Nothing but grief befalls those whom Fortune does
>   not favor,
> And black death comes in a thousand calamitous ways.)

2. An alphabetical list of the forty-three names is given in Delmarcel 1981, p. 701.

EXHIBITIONS
Exposición Histórico-Europea, Madrid, 1893
"Cinq Siècles d'art," Brussels, 1935
La Galería del Príncipe, Palacio Real, Madrid, 1964
"Tapisseries des maisons royales d'Espagne," Bordeaux, 1968

OPPOSITE: Vulcan, god of fire and metal working (detail of cat. 1, upper right). To the left is Amphion, Niobe's husband, who committed suicide for grief at the loss of their many sons and daughters, all slain by Apollo.

Danaë cast out to sea with Perseus, her son by Jupiter (detail of cat. 1, lower left of center). Rescued, Danaë had a happier fate than Hero, who drowned herself in the Hellespont for love of Leander, drowned in the same sea. Above Danaë is Polycrates of Samos, a Greek tyrant whose life of great good fortune came to an ignominious end, as a result of treachery, in 522 B.C. To temper his good fortune in the eyes of the gods, Polycrates is said to have thrown a treasured signet ring into the sea, only to have it returned soon after in the innards of a prize catch presented to him by a fisherman.

Paupertas, or Poverty, decrying her lot (detail of cat. 1, to the lower right). Surrounding her are examples of the great brought low by Fortune: Priam, king of Troy, Cleopatra, and the Roman lawgiver Appius Claudius. Romilda, whose robe appears above, was a Lombard princess who betrayed Cividale del Friuli to the Avars and was impaled by them for her pains.

OPPOSITE: Phoebus Apollo, god of the sun, of archery, and of music, attended by Flora, goddess of flowers and the spring, and Zephyrus, the west wind (detail of cat. 1, upper left). Among the figures below them are Julius Caesar being rowed to shore and Melantho, who after an affair with Poseidon in the guise of a dolphin, gave birth to Delphus, founder of Delphi.

2 Fame

Los Honores: sixth tapestry
Workshop of Pieter van Aelst (active 1495–1531), after a
cartoon attributed to Bernaert van Orley (ca. 1491–1541/42)
Brussels, 1520–23
Gold, silver, silk, and wool
16 ft. 6 in. x 33 ft. 8 in. (505 x 1030 cm.)
Segovia, Museo de Tapices, Palacio de San Ildefonso
Inv. PN. S.8/3

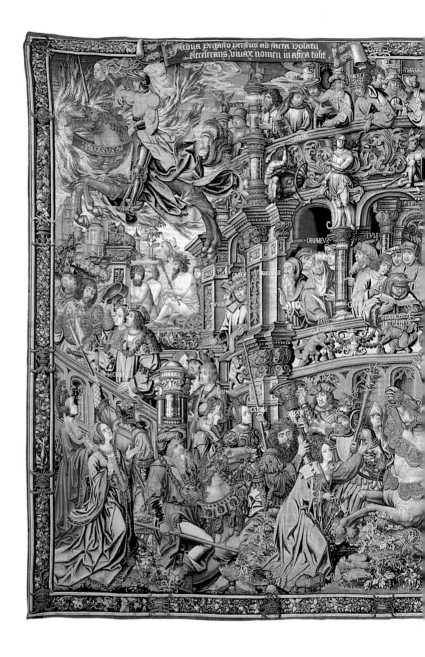

In the center of an edifice with two projecting double
balconies the female personification of Fame is seated
astride an elephant and blows two trumpets. To the
left, the valiant Perseus is mounted upon the winged
horse Pegasus, symbol of Good Repute. To the right,
Bad Repute, a monstrous creature as described by Vir-
gil, is winging her way over the sea.

Good and bad repute are transmitted through the
work of writers; hence it is they, from Homer to
Valerius Maximus, who fill the balconies of the Palace
of Fame. The place of honor, in the first row on the
left, has been reserved for Petrarch, whose *Trionfi*
(Triumphs) is considered to have been a source of inspiration for the set. As in the other tapestries of *Los
Honores*, the allegorical, biblical, and historical figures
represented are identified by their names.[3]

Along the upper edge, the border of flowers and
fruit incorporates three scrolls bearing Latin inscriptions:

Ardua Pegaseo Perseus ad facta volatu
Accelerans, vivax nomen in astra tulit.

(Hastening with the flight of Pegasus toward lofty deeds,
Perseus carried his enduring name to the stars.)

Fama vel effractis reuocat quoscu[m]q[ue] sepulchris
Hinc laudes illinc probra caue[n]te [canente] tuba.

(After tombs are broken open, Fame recalls whom she
will,
The trumpet sounding praises here, reproaches there.)

Mendax fama viros urbes pallacia reges
Territat horrendi nu[n]cia prompta mali.

(Deceitful rumor, prompt messenger of dreadful ill,
Spreads fear among men, cities, mistresses, kings.)

---

3. Delmarcel 1981, pp. 705–706, lists a total of eighty names.

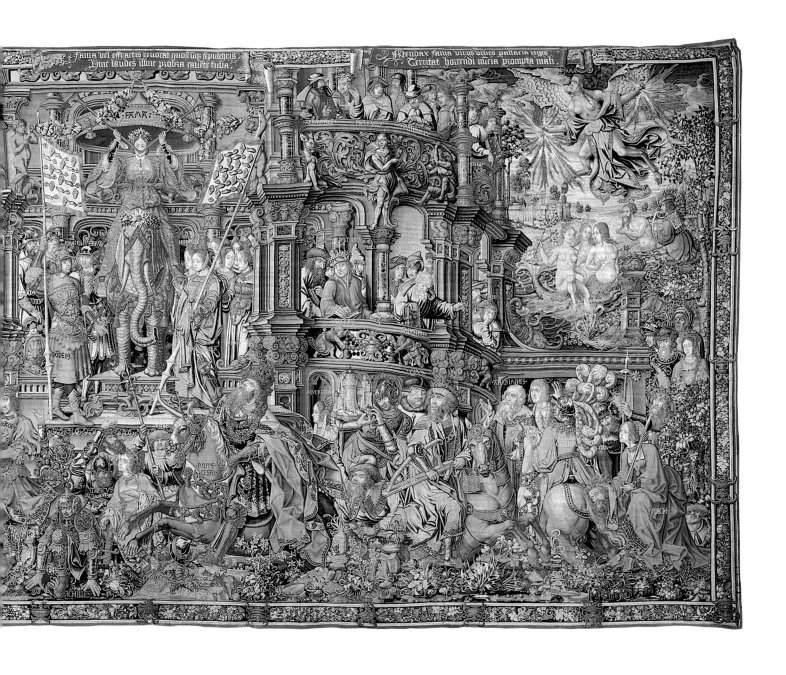

EXHIBITION

La Galería del Príncipe, Palacio Real, Madrid, 1964

LITERATURE

Madrazo 1889, cuaderno 3, "La Fama," n.p., pl. 17; Valencia de
Don Juan 1903, I, pp. 23–24, II, pls. 32–40, esp. 34, 36; Tormo
Monzó and Sánchez Cantón 1919, pp. 51–54, pls. XIX, XX;
Saintenoy 1921, p. 18; Göbel 1923, I:1, pp. 118–123; Crick-
Kuntziger 1935, pp. 47–50, 64–68, nos. 622, 623; Steppe 1968,
pp. 720–734; Delmarcel 1979; Delmarcel 1981, pp. 281–326
(*Fortune*), 441–474 (*Fame*); Junquera de Vega and Herrero
Carretero 1986, pp. 35–44, esp. pp. 38, 40.

OPPOSITE: Fame, with her two trumpets (detail of cat. 2,
upper center). Her banners—all eyes and ears and tongues—
are held by Pompey the Great on the left and, on the right,
by Penthesilea, the Amazon queen who came to the aid of
Troy and was killed by Achilles. Roland and Oliver, heroes of
Roncesvalles, are in the group on the left, Hippolyta, queen
of the Amazons, and Dido, queen of Carthage, on the right.

BELOW: Proteus, Neptune's herdsman and a prophet, able
to assume a different shape at will, with a group of sea
goddesses: Arethusa, Thetis, mother of Achilles (she took on
the guise of a dolphin in an attempt to escape the advances
of Peleus), and improbably, Glaucus, in fact a fisherman who
became a sea god with the gift of prophecy (detail of cat. 2,
upper right). On the right is the Greek lyric poet Arion, said
to have been rescued from the sea by a dolphin.

Ardua Pegaseo Perseus ad facta
Accelerans, viuax nomen m

PEGASVS

PERSEVS

BOCACE

PROMPRIDE

OVIDE

OMERE

HECTOR

MARCIA

OPPOSITE: Riding to their places among the stars are Perseus, bearing the head of Medusa, and the winged horse Pegasus (detail of cat. 2, upper left). Below them are Neptune, god of the sea, Hector of Troy, Marcia (wife of Regulus?), and the Trojan soothsayer Helenus. On the right, looking out from the upper gallery of the Palace of Fame, are the authors Boccaccio and Pronapides (an Athenian said to have been Homer's teacher and to have introduced the left-to-right system of writing); Homer and Ovid are in the lower gallery.

LEFT: Socrates, Demosthenes, and the 1st-century B.C. Roman historian Pompeius Trogus (detail of cat. 2, upper right)

BELOW: Julius Caesar (detail of cat. 2, lower right of center), with Theseus, Penelope, and Jason on the left, and Lucretia on the right. At lower right is the turbaned Muhammad.

The Apocalypse

New sets of tapestries acquired during the reign of Philip II included the spectacular *Apocalypse* sequence, woven with gold, silver, silk, and wool thread.

Although the designs go back to an earlier time, the purchase of eight tapestries representing the Apocalypse of St. John is first mentioned in a document dating probably from 1553.[1] With the exception of two of the tapestries, this set was lost in a storm, along with other furnishings of the royal bedchamber, during the king's disembarkation at Laredo, near Santander, on September 8, 1559. Philip then ordered replicas of the missing tapestries to be woven by his tapestry maker Willem de Pannemaker, under the supervision of Antoine Perrenot de Granvelle (1517–1586). (Adviser to the regent of the Netherlands, Granvelle, who was named cardinal in 1561, was himself a collector of Flemish tapestries; see page 83.) When the work was completed, Pannemaker personally delivered to Madrid the six tapestries he had woven, together with the two spared in the disaster of 1559, which had no doubt been entrusted to him as a guide in making the replacements. From that time on the tapestries that had been rescued from the sea were registered in the royal inventories as *Los ahogados*, the "drowned ones."[2] Pannemaker's journey from Brussels began in the summer of 1561 and ended in Madrid on October 22 of that year.[3]

Marthe Crick-Kuntziger believed that Bernaert van Orley was the author of the cartoons, which he had based on prints by Albrecht Dürer (1471–1528). Some of the motifs in the series, however, do not appear in Dürer's *Apocalypse*. Scenes depicted in the sixth tapestry, for example, correspond with none of Dürer's designs, and other passages are treated with considerable license. Dürer's *Apocalypse*, illustrating a condensed version of the book of Revelation, comprises fifteen woodcuts; the first printing in 1498 was published in two editions, one with a German text, the other in Latin. According to Erwin Panofsky, "Dürer's compositions were copied, not only in Germany, but also in Italy, in France and in Russia, and not only in woodcuts and engravings but also in paintings, reliefs, tapestries, and enamels. Their indirect influence, transmitted by a master like Holbein, as well as by such modest craftsmen as the illustrators of the Luther Bibles, reached even the monasteries of Mount Athos."[4]

The composition of the tapestries, like the design of Dürer's woodcuts, is dominated by a vertical axis and a strong horizontal division, with the various scenes organized in contiguous registers. The eight tapestries depict the seven great apocalyptic visions narrated in the twenty-two chapters of the Revelation of St. John the Divine: *St. John on Patmos* (Rev. 1–5); *The Four Horsemen of the Apocalypse* (Rev. 6–7); *The Adoration of the Lamb* (Rev. 7–10); *St. John Ordered to Measure the Temple* (Rev. 11–12); *St. Michael Overcoming Satan* (Rev. 12–14); *The Angel Bearing the Gospel* (Rev. 14–16); *The Marriage of the Lamb* (Rev. 16–19); *The Angel Overcoming the Dragon* (Rev. 19–22).

1. "Relación de los ocho paños de la historia de san Juan Apocalipsis que su magestad mandó tomar de Diric de Madenar y Gaspar van Utreque." Archivo General de Simancas, Estado, legajo 98, fol. 48; see Beer 1891, p. CV.
2. See Gloria Fernández Bayton, *Inventarios Reales: Testamentaria del Rey Carlos II, 1701–1703* (Madrid: Museo del Prado, 1975) I, p. 245.
3. "Cuenta de Pannemaker por conducir la tapicería del Apocalipsis de Flandes a España, en 1561." Archivo General de Simancas, Casa y Sitios Reales, legajo 251, fol. 123; see Steppe 1981a, pp. 121–124.
4. Erwin Panofsky, *The Life and Art of Albrecht Dürer*, 4th ed. (Princeton, N.J.: Princeton University Press, 1955) p. 59.

OPPOSITE: "And there was war in heaven: Michael and his angels fought against the dragon" (detail of cat. 4, upper left).

3 *The Adoration of the Lamb*

The Apocalypse: third tapestry
Workshop of Willem de Pannemaker (active 1535–78), after a
cartoon attributed to Bernaert van Orley (ca. 1491–1541/42)
Brussels, 1560–61
Weaver's mark
Gold, silver, silk, and wool
17 ft. 4 in. x 28 ft. 9 in. (530 x 880 cm.)
Segovia, Museo de Tapices, Palacio de San Ildefonso
Inv. PN. S.11/3

After this I beheld, and lo, a great multitude, which no
man could number, of all nations, and kindreds, and
people, and tongues, stood before the throne, and before the Lamb, clothed with white robes, and palms in
their hands;

And cried with a loud voice, saying, Salvation to our
God which sitteth upon the throne, and unto the Lamb.

And all the angels stood round about the throne, and
about the elders and the four beasts, and fell before the
throne on their faces, and worshipped God,

Saying, Amen. (Revelation 7:9–12)

The third tapestry in the set depicts chapters 7 through
10 of the Revelation of St. John, who is shown kneeling in the center foreground. Above, the multitude of
the elect, palms in hand, are crying out the praises of
the Lamb, which is surrounded by the four beasts traditionally symbolizing the Evangelists, by angels, and
by the twenty-four elders; one of the elders is collect-
ing in a chalice the blood that flows from the Lamb.
To the left of this scene, seven angels receive from
God the seven trumpets of the Last Judgment; another angel is about to cast the censer down to earth.

In the lower left half of the tapestry, fire and blood
rain down upon the earth; a blazing mountain is cast
into the sea; the star "called Wormwood" drops into
the poisoned waters; the sun and moon are darkened.
A star falls from the sky with the key to the bottom-
less pit, out of which swarm locusts with horses' bodies, human faces, lions' teeth, and scorpions' tails.

To the right of the Lamb, the voice from heaven is
symbolized by four masks, one on each corner of the
"golden altar which is before God"; above the altar is
a vision of God, shown head and shoulders. At his
command the angel with the trumpet sounds it to un-
leash the four avenging angels from the river Euphra-
tes. It is these angels who are seen in the lower right

The Lamb adored (detail of cat. 3, upper center)

OPPOSITE: St. John on Patmos (detail of cat. 3, lower center)

of the tapestry, brandishing their swords against "the third part of men." Above them is an army mounted on horses with serpents' tails and with lions' heads breathing fire, smoke, and brimstone. To the right of this army is the angel "clothed with a cloud," with a radiant face and feet like pillars of fire, straddling land and sea; he is handing the book to John, who is devouring it.

The border of flowers around the trunk of a palm tree is interspersed with birds and animals. A cartouche in the upper border contains the Latin inscription:

HOC.EVANGELII.RESONAT.TVBA.MISSA.PER.ORBEM
HOC.ET.APOSTOLICO.DOGMATE.TEMPLA.SONANT.
ET.SANCTA.ERRORES.VARIOS.DOCTRINA.REPELLIT
VERVS.AMOR.FIDIS.MENTIBVS.INSERITVR.

(With this the trumpet of the Gospel resounds
    throughout the world,
And temples echo with this apostolic doctrine.
And sacred teaching drives off divers errors;
True love is planted in faithful minds.)

EXHIBITIONS
International Exposition, Brussels, 1935, no. 625
Eucharistic Congress, Barcelona, 1952

The angel "clothed with a cloud" presenting the book to St. John (detail of cat. 3, upper right)

OPPOSITE: Detail of the avenging angels (cat. 3, to the lower right)

4 *St. Michael Overcoming Satan*

The Apocalypse: fifth tapestry
Workshop of Jan Gheteels (active 1530–54), after a cartoon
attributed to Bernaert van Orley (ca. 1491–1541/42)
Brussels, ca. 1550
Weaver's mark and the *B*'s of Brabant–Brussels
Gold, silver, silk, and wool
17 ft. 2 in. x 27 ft. 9 in. (525 x 850 cm.)
Segovia, Museo de Tapices, Palacio de San Ildefonso
Inv. PN. S.11/5

And there was war in heaven: Michael and his angels
fought against the dragon; and the dragon fought and
his angels,

   And prevailed not; neither was their place found any
more in heaven.

   And the great dragon was cast out, that old serpent,
called the Devil, and Satan, which deceiveth the whole
world: he was cast out into the earth, and his angels
were cast out with him. (Revelation 12:7–9)

The fifth tapestry in the series represents events described in Revelation 12:7–14:5. Woven in the workshop of Jan Gheteels, this is one of the two pieces of
the original set that were rescued from the shipwreck
of 1559.

   God is seated on his throne on high, surrounded
by the four beasts and the twenty-four elders. Below
them are the beast risen from the sea, identified as
BLASPHEMIA, and the dragon, with its adorers, over
whose heads is the inscription: QVIS SIMILIS BESTIE
ET QVIS POTERIT PVGNARE CVN EA ("Who is like
unto the beast? who is able to make war with him?"
Rev. 13:4).

   To the left is the archangel Michael, accompanied
by his angels: he is battling the dragon—SATANAS—
and triumphing over him. In the center foreground,
an angel places the wings of an eagle on the woman
crowned with stars, who is being pursued by the
dragon; above, and to the left, she rises in flight, es-
caping the river that the dragon vomits up in a vain
attempt to sweep her away.

   To the right, in the foreground, the beast risen
from the sea, with its seven heads, ten horns, and ten
crowns, is hurling itself against an army. In the middle ground, the beast come from the earth causes fire
to rain down upon men, who are forced, whatever

SATANAS

their condition, to adore the beast from the sea; the latter's image, raised on a column, is being worshiped by a group of figures that includes a kneeling king and bishop. In the upper right is the Lamb, standing on Mount Sion, surrounded by the faithful singing a "new song."

The cartouche in the upper border contains the Latin inscription:

CERTA·QVIES·NVMQ[VAM]· VIRTVTI·EST·INVIDIOS[A]E
AD·FINEM·S(A)EC[V]LI·ILLAM·PREMET·VSQ[VE]·LABOR·
NV[M]Q[VAM]·SVCCVMBET·SPE·FORTI TVTAFIDEQV[E]
QVAMVIS·IVSSA·DEI·RISERIT·IMPIETAS·

(There is no certain rest for envied virtue.
Struggle is her burden even to the end of time.
With strong hope and sure faith she never falters,
No matter how great the impiety that mocks the
    commands of God.)

LITERATURE

Wittert 1876; Madrazo 1880, pp. 283–419; Madrazo 1889, cuaderno I, "El Apocalipsis," n.p., pl. 4; Beer 1891, p. CV; Valencia de Don Juan 1903, I, pp. 65–67, II, pls. 82–89, esp. 84, 86; Tormo Monzó and Sánchez Cantón 1919, pp. 57–62, pls. XXII–XXIV; Göbel 1923, I:1, pp. 156–158, 417, I:2, pls. 128, 129; Crick-Kuntziger 1935, pp. 68–71, nos. 624–626; Crick-Kuntziger 1943, pp. 84–86; Crick-Kuntziger 1956; Steppe 1968, pp. 734–748; Steppe 1981a; Herrero Carretero 1986; Junquera de Vega and Herrero Carretero 1986, pp. 54–62, esp. pp. 57, 59.

OPPOSITE: "And the great dragon was cast out, that old serpent, called the Devil" (detail of cat. 4, left).

BELOW: The beast risen from the sea attacks an army (detail of cat. 4, lower right).

LEFT: Worshiping the beast that had come up out of the earth (detail of cat. 4, upper right)

BELOW: Detail of the border (cat. 4, lower center)

"And to the woman were given two wings of a great eagle" (detail of cat. 4, lower center).

The Spheres

The representation of the celestial sphere, conceived according to the Ptolemaic system, indicates that the set was woven before 1543, the year of the publication of *De revolutionibus orbium coelestium*, in which Nicolaus Copernicus made known to the world the heliocentric system of astronomy.

The tapestries exalt the heroic exploits of the Portuguese navigators under the patronage of the monarchs of the house of Aviz. They were commissioned by King John III of Portugal (1502–1557), no doubt with the intention of commemorating the voyages of discovery begun in the time of his forebears Prince Henry the Navigator (1394–1460) and King Alfonso V (1432–1481), the African. It is not known precisely when the tapestries became part of the collection of the Spanish crown, but it may well have been in 1543, the year Philip II married Maria of Portugal, daughter of John III.

Woven in Brussels during the third decade of the sixteenth century, the set consists of three hangings, each of which represents a different sphere: celestial, armillary, and terrestrial. In the 1880 inventory of the royal tapestries, a fourth piece, *Coriolanus Before Rome with Veturia and Volumnia*, was listed with the set as having the same height and borders.

A mark, still not positively identified, is woven in gold on the right guard border of the tapestries: it consists of an upright with a broad leaf on either side in the lower part, a floral wreath in the center, and a pennant at the top. The same mark appears on the *editio princeps* of *Vertumnus and Pomona*, a set acquired by Charles V from the weaver or merchant Georg Wezeler.

The skillful composition and vigorous design of the tapestries suggest that the cartoons that served as models may be attributed to the Italian-influenced painter Bernaert van Orley. Van Orley's brothers Everard and Gomar were employed in his workshop, as well as numerous assistants; some specialized in landscape, others in plants and flowers, and others again in the creation of borders. It is possible, therefore, that the master drew upon this multiple collaboration in designing the *Spheres*.

OPPOSITE: Hercules and the celestial sphere (detail of cat. 5, center)

Detail of the border, with an armillary sphere (cat. 5, upper left of center)

5 *Hercules Supporting the Celestial Sphere*

The Spheres: first tapestry
Woven by or at the order of Georg Wezeler, after a cartoon
attributed to Bernaert van Orley (ca. 1491–1541/42)
Brussels, ca. 1520–30
Mark of the weaver or merchant
Gold, silver, silk, and wool
11 ft. 3 in. x 10 ft. 1 in. (345 x 308 cm.)
Madrid, Palacio Real
Inv. PN. S.15/1

The celestial sphere, occupying the center of the composition, is held up by Hercules, partly cloaked in the skin of the Nemean lion. In place of Atlas, he bears the weight of the firmament, as if he were a column sustaining the vault of the heavens. On either side of the Theban hero stands a group of three figures. One of the two women on the left is holding—as if to prevent its flight—the shaft of an arrow that Cupid, at their feet, has not yet put to his bow. Some have seen in this group an allegory of blind and instinctive love as opposed to love governed by reason and reflection. On the other side Mercury announces to an embracing Mars and Venus the vengeance that Vulcan, wounded by his wife's infidelity, plots against them.

In the upper corners are representations of human destiny and toil. Destiny, on the left, is personified by a winged figure, who with a quill draws the signs of the zodiac on the celestial sphere, while an eagle holds a laurel wreath above his head. The young laborer on the right, zealously digging with his spade, symbolizes man's toil, which, as represented by a winged head and a star, lasts from dawn to dusk.

The border of flowers and fruit around a central stem, interspersed with animals and ribbons, is characteristic of Flemish tapestries of the first half of the sixteenth century. The scroll in the upper border contains the Latin inscription:

MAGNA VIRTVS, SED
ALIENAE OBNOXIA.

(Great is virtue,
But at the mercy of another.)

EXHIBITIONS
"Carlos V y su ambiente," Toledo, 1958
"Los descubrimientos portugueses y la Europa del Renacimiento,"
17th European Exhibition of Art, Science, and Culture, Lisbon,
1983

Man's toil (detail of cat. 5, upper right)

6 *Atlas Supporting the Armillary Sphere*

The Spheres: second tapestry
Woven by or at the order of Georg Wezeler, after a cartoon
attributed to Bernaert van Orley (ca. 1491–1541/42)
Brussels, ca. 1520–30
Mark of the weaver or merchant
Gold, silver, silk, and wool
11 ft. 2 in. x 11 ft. 4 in. (342 x 348 cm.)
Madrid, Palacio Real
Inv. PN. S.15/2

Atlas, kneeling, is at the center of the composition;
with muscular arms he raises the armillary sphere—
showing the principal circles of the celestial sphere—
high above his head. On the left are two allegorical
figures: Aurora, crowned with flowers and radiant
beams of light, her arms lifted toward the heavens and
her great wings extended; and the Moon, growing
pale in the light of dawn, with a crescent moon and a
star above her head and a crab—Cancer, symbol of
the moon and the fourth sign of the zodiac—at her
feet. To the right are the Hours, four maidens who
pour water from their amphoras to form the current
of time. On the ground before them is a dragon, a
winged reptile, symbol of the sun.

In the upper corners are Mercury, with a caduceus,
and Urania, muse of astronomy, holding in one hand
an armillary sphere mounted on a pole.

The scroll in the upper border contains the Latin
inscription:

INGENS FAMA, SED
ALTERIVS, EA EST, IGEPS [?INOPS].

(Vast is fame,
But powerless, being another's.)

EXHIBITIONS
"Carlos V y su ambiente," Toledo, 1958
"Los descubrimientos portugueses y la Europa del Renacimiento,"
17th European Exhibition of Art, Science, and Culture, Lisbon,
1983

A dragon, symbol of the sun (detail of cat. 6, lower right)

OPPOSITE: Aurora confronting the Moon (detail of cat. 6, left)

RIGHT: The Hours pouring water to form the current of time (detail of cat. 6, right)

61

7 Earth Under the Protection of Jupiter and Juno

The Spheres: third tapestry
Woven by or at the order of Georg Wezeler, after a cartoon
attributed to Bernaert van Orley (ca. 1491–1541/42)
Brussels, ca. 1520–30
Mark of the weaver or merchant
Gold, silver, silk, and wool
11 ft. 3 in. x 10 ft. 3 in. (344 x 314 cm.)
Madrid, Palacio Real
Inv. PN. S.15/3

The terrestrial sphere is encircled by winged heads, symbols of the winds. Jupiter, crowned and with a scepter in one hand, and Juno, crowned and holding a scepter tipped by a fleur-de-lis, extend their protection over the globe. God and goddess each stand on a strip of cloth supported by a winged figure. The globe shows Africa and the East Indies, regions that were the scene of great exploits and discoveries by Portuguese navigators. Specific locations are marked with the arms of Portugal, which has prompted speculation that the principal figures represent King John III and his wife, Catherine of Austria. The sun above and the moon below the terrestrial sphere define the vertical axis of a markedly symmetrical composition. In the upper corners are the symbolic figures of Abundance and Wisdom on the left and of Fame and Victory on the right.

The scroll in the upper border is inscribed:

GLORIA SVMMA,
NAM SVA IPSIVS SOLA.

(Glory is supreme,
For it issues from itself alone.)

EXHIBITIONS
"A la découverte du monde," Bordeaux, 1960
"Los descubrimientos portugueses y la Europa del Renacimiento,"
17th European Exhibition of Art, Science, and Culture, Lisbon
1983
"Splendeur d'Espagne et des villes belges, 1500–1700" (Europalia
85 España), Brussels, 1985

LITERATURE
Madrazo 1889, cuaderno 1, "Hércules sosteniendo la esfera celeste,"
n.p., pl. 3; Calvert 1921, pp. 66–67, pls. 114, 115; Göbel 1923, I:1,
pp. 145–146, 417, I:2, pls. 113, 114; Toledo 1958, p. 240, no. 645,
pl. CCXXX; Martin-Méry 1960, p. 96, no. 176, pl. 1; Junquera
1973a; Duverger 1985; Junquera de Vega and Herrero Carretero
1986, pp. 100–103.

The winged figure supporting Juno (detail of cat. 7, lower right)

The winged figure supporting Jupiter (detail of cat. 7, lower left)

PAGES 64 AND 65: Jupiter and Juno (details of cat. 7, left and right), perhaps representing King John III of Portugal, who commissioned the *Spheres* tapestries, and his queen, Catherine of Austria

OPPOSITE: The globe, showing Africa and the East Indies. Flags with the arms of Portugal mark the sites of Portuguese discoveries (detail of cat. 7, center).

The Story of Scipio

The *editio princeps* of this series was commissioned in 1532 by Francis I of France, after designs by Giulio Romano, the pupil of Raphael. It consisted of a total of twenty-two tapestries depicting the exploits and the triumph of Scipio Africanus, as recounted in the histories of Rome written by Livy (59 B.C.–A.D. 17) and the second-century Greek Appian. Twelve tapestries represented major events in the Second Punic War, from the battle of Ticinum to the decisive battle of Zama. The remaining ten featured scenes of Scipio's triumph on his return to Rome, culminating in the public feast with which victorious commanders were honored. This set, woven with gold and silver thread, was deliberately burned in the decade following the French Revolution in order to recover its metal content.

In 1544 Mary of Austria (1505–1558), queen of Hungary from 1522 to 1526 and regent of the Netherlands for her brother Charles V, acquired a seven-piece set of the *Story of Scipio* from the Antwerp merchant Erasmus Schatz. It was inventoried by the queen's treasurer, Rogier Patie, between 1555 and 1558, and bequeathed, according to a marginal note in the same inventory, to her nephew Philip II.[1] Since that time it has remained in the tapestry collection of the Spanish crown. With the destruction of the *editio princeps* in 1797, it is the oldest set to have survived.

Five episodes of the Second Punic War are depicted: *The Taking of New Carthage* (Cartagena); *The Continence of Scipio; The Capture of Hasdrubal's Camp; The Meeting of Scipio and Hannibal;* and *The Battle of Zama;*[2] and two scenes from the triumph of Scipio as described in book 8 of Appian's history of Rome: *Oxen and Elephants* and *The Banquet*.[3]

The composition of these tapestries follows exactly the preparatory sketches executed by Giulio Romano in 1528, in collaboration with Giovan Francesco Penni, for the set commissioned by Francis I and woven in the Brussels workshop of van der Moyen.

The only marks on Mary of Hungary's set are the *B*'s of Brabant–Brussels on the *Battle of Zama* and an undeciphered weaver's mark, resembling a chandelier or ship, on the guard border of the *Capture of Hasdrubal's Camp*. The same mark has been attributed to Erasmus Schatz, the merchant involved in the purchase of the tapestries.

Roman infantry brandishing torches and sowing panic among Hannibal's elephants (detail of cat. 8, to the lower left)

OPPOSITE: One of Hannibal's elephants under attack (detail of cat. 8, right of center)

1. Archivo General de Simancas, Contaduría mayor, primera época, legajo 1017; see Beer 1891, pp. CLVIII–CLXIV, esp. p. CLX.
2. Inv. PN. S.26/1–5.
3. Inv. PN. S.26/6, 7.

8 *The Battle of Zama*

The Story of Scipio: fifth tapestry
Workshop unknown, after a cartoon by Giulio Romano
(1499–1546)
Brussels, ca. 1544
Mark of Brabant–Brussels
Silk and wool
15 ft. 7 in. x 29 ft. 6 in. (480 x 902 cm.)
Madrid, Palacio Real
Inv. PN. S.26/5

One of the most important episodes in the Second
Punic War, the battle of Zama was fought in 202 B.C.
in what is today Tunisia, between the Romans under
the command of their general, Publius Cornelius
Scipio (234–183), and the Carthaginians, led by Hannibal (247–183/2). The battle is narrated in book 30,
chapters 33–35, of Livy's history of Rome.

In the foreground, the composition depicts the
Roman cavalry led by Laelius and a Numidian
company under the command of Masinissa, a Carthaginian deserter. The Romans launched the engagement by yelling a thunderous war cry that spread
panic among the elephants Hannibal had arrayed in
his front line, in advance of his infantry. The rout of
the elephants, shown in the middle ground, as they
were thrown back upon Hannibal's Numidian cavalry, decided Scipio's victory in the battle, which won
him the name Africanus, the African. The hand-to-
hand fighting between Romans and Carthaginians is
depicted in scenes of great violence, such as that of
the two combatants in the center foreground who are
grappling on the ground, one biting the other's nose,
a spectacle repeated in the *Battle of Ticinum* in another set owned by the Patrimonio Nacional.[4]

Two of Giulio Romano's preparatory sketches for
the *Battle of Zama* are in the Cabinet des Dessins in
the Louvre (inv. 3717, 3718), and the Ashmolean Museum, Oxford, has a sheet with four studies of an
elephant.[5]

The border of volutes, candelabra, griffins, and a
carved, gilded frame on a blue background is similar
to that of the tapestries in the *Story of Noah*, a set
woven in the Brussels workshop of Joost van Herselle
for the same patron, Mary of Hungary.[6]

4. Inv. PN. S.28/1.

5. K. T. Parker, *Catalogue of the Collection of Drawings in the Ashmolean Museum*: II. *Italian Schools* (Oxford, 1956) pp. 322–323, no. 590.

6. Inv. PN. S.24/1–7.

EXHIBITIONS

Exposición Ibero-Americana, Seville, 1929

"La Universidad en el Renacimiento," Hospital Real, Granada, 1982

Exposición Histórico-Europea, Madrid, 1983

LITERATURE

Guiffrey 1877, esp. pp. 283–284; Dollmayr 1901; Valencia de Don Juan 1903, I, p. 69, II, pls. 90–96; Astier 1907, pp. 148–149, 150–152, pls. v, xxvIII, xxIx, xxxII; Tormo Monzó and Sánchez Cantón 1919, pp. 69–73, pl. xxvII; Calvert 1921, pp. 89–98, pls. 91–93; Göbel 1923, I:1, p. 166, I:2, pl. 78; Asselberghs 1971, nos. 9, 10; Schneebalg-Perelman 1971, pp. 261–262; Junquera 1973b; Paris 1978, pp. 27, 38, 43, 50, 71, 89, 98, 119, 139, 148; Junquera de Vega and Herrero Carretero 1986, pp. 176–184, esp. p. 182; Forti Grazzini 1989, pp. 467–473.

OPPOSITE: The Carthaginians hard pressed by Roman cavalry and foot soldiers (detail of cat. 8, upper right)

BELOW: The fallen comrade (detail of cat. 8, lower left)

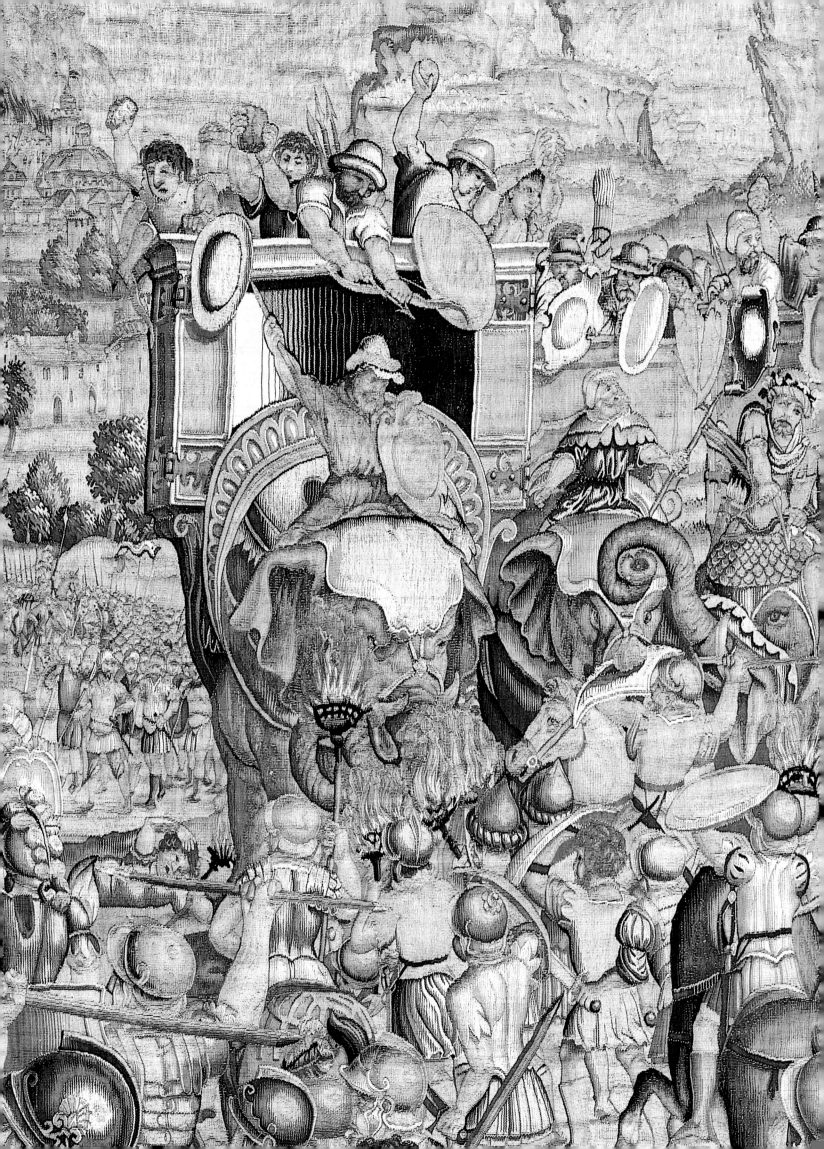

The Conquest of Tunis

Charles V, Holy Roman Emperor, and, as Charles I, king of Spain, commissioned the weaving of the *Conquest of Tunis* to commemorate his expedition against the Turks, which was undertaken in 1535. The Flemish artists Jan Cornelisz Vermeyen and Pieter Coecke van Aelst accompanied the emperor in order to make sketches from life that would later serve as the basis of the cartoons for the tapestries. The presence of the two painters on the expedition is corroborated by their self-portraits in the cartoon and tapestry depicting the Sack of Tunis: two men, bearded but still young, are observing the scenes of war while one of them sketches in a large album.

Jan Cornelisz Vermeyen, also known as Juan de Majo, was first attached to the court of Margaret of Austria (1480–1530), regent of the Netherlands for her nephew Charles V. In 1534 Vermeyen was summoned to Spain to serve the emperor, in his capacity as both engineer and artist. It was he who was to be responsible for painting the individuals who took part in the historic expedition, while Pieter Coecke van Aelst was to record the architectural features and landscape, all faithfully represented in the novel aerial perspectives of the cartoons. These are today in the Kunsthistorisches Museum in Vienna.[1]

The Conquest of Tunis was the most costly set of tapestries commissioned by Charles V. On February 20, 1548, Willem de Pannemaker signed the contract binding him to produce this series, using Granada silks, fine wool and worsted thread from Lyons, and thread of gold and silver that was to be provided by the emperor himself. The twelve enormous pieces of the set measure in all approximately 600 square meters. Executing the cartoons, composing the in-

scriptions, and weaving the tapestries took years of work—from 1546 to 1554.[2]

In 1731, in order to ensure the preservation of the *editio princeps*, Philip V, the first Bourbon king of Spain, ordered that a duplicate set be woven in the Real Fábrica de Tapices de Santa Barbara de Madrid, the royal tapestry works established in the capital under the auspices of Cardinal Alberoni and directed by members of the van der Goten family of weavers from Antwerp. The twelve tapestries were completed in 1744 and delivered, by royal order, on September 28 of the same year to the Tapestry Office.

It is because of the replicas made at Philip's instigation that we know the design of the eighth (*The Battle of the Tunisian Wells*) and eleventh (*The Army Encamped at Rada*) pieces of the original Brussels, or "old" *Tunis*, set. The two were later lost after having been in the possession of the widowed queen of Spain, Maria Anna of Bavaria-Neuburg (1667–1740), in Toledo and Guadalajara.[3] In the inventory of the will of Ferdinand VII (1834), the set was listed as consisting of ten tapestries.[4]

The military and naval expedition launched by Charles V in the western Mediterranean in 1535 against the famous corsair Barbarossa, Khayr ad-Din, and the might of the Turkish sultan, Suleyman the Magnificent, ended with the capture of La Goleta, and of Tunis itself, on July 21 of that year. The ten surviving tapestries in the *princeps* set are: *The Map; The Review of the Troops at Barcelona; The Landing at La Goleta; The Attack on La Goleta; The Naval Battle off La Goleta; The Enemy Sortie from La Goleta; The Taking of La Goleta; The Taking of Tunis; The Sack of Tunis; The Reembarkation of the Army at La Goleta.*

OPPOSITE: Traditionally identified as Dom Luis, infante of Portugal, this youth may instead be the page of the horseman preceding him, the duke of Alba (detail of cat. 9, center foreground).

1. *Historischen Schlachten auf Tapisseries aus dem Besitz des Kunsthistorischen Museums Wien*, exh. cat., Schloss Halbturn (Vienna, 1976) pp. 15–28. See also Horn 1989.
2. Houdoy 1873, pp. 15–19.
3. Archivo de Palacio, Sección Histórica: Fernando VI, legajo 19.
4. "Testamentaria del Señor don Fernando 7º de Borbón. Año de 1834. Tomo 1º." Archivo de Palacio, Registros, 4807.

9 *The Review of the Troops at Barcelona*

The Conquest of Tunis: second tapestry
Workshop of Willem de Pannemaker (active 1535–78), after a
cartoon by Jan Cornelisz Vermeyen (1500–1559) and Pieter
Coecke van Aelst (1502–1550)
Brussels, 1546–54
Weaver's mark and the *B*'s of Brabant–Brussels
Gold, silver, silk, and wool
17 ft. 2 in. x 23 ft. 4 in. (525 x 712 cm.)
Madrid, Palacio Real
Inv. PN. S.13/2

The painters of the cartoons overcame the repetitious-
ness of the military scenes by placing the line of the
horizon high in the design and filling the foreground
with precisely rendered incident. For the sake of even
greater clarity, essential facts are related in explanatory inscriptions in Spanish and Latin in the upper
and lower borders respectively.

This second tapestry in the series represents the ar-
rival of the emperor in Barcelona at the head of his
army, and his review of the forces brought by Portuguese caravels under Antonio de Saldaña, Genoese
galleys commanded by Admiral Andrea Doria, and
the Castilian ships of the famous seaman Alvaro de
Bazán.

The emperor, who had arrived in Barcelona on
April 3, 1535, held a general muster on May 14. The
parade of the different companies of Spanish, German, Italian, Neapolitan, and Portuguese knights
took place on the field of La Laguna, outside the port
of Perpignan. Recognizable among the most eminent
figures are the Portuguese infante Dom Luis,[5] brother
of the empress, and the duke of Alba. In the middle
distance is Charles V himself, holding a mace of
gilded iron and arrayed in full armor—except for his
head, covered only by a visored cap. Similarly prominent is the knight carrying the Genoese standard, a
crimson pennant displaying the Virgin and Child.

The scene is framed by a border of interlocking circles with the imperial double eagle and arms of the
monarch in the upper corners, and a wreath of
flowers surrounding the Burgundian cross and fire-
steel in the lower. The columns of Hercules and the
motto of Charles V in French, *Plus Oultre*, appear in

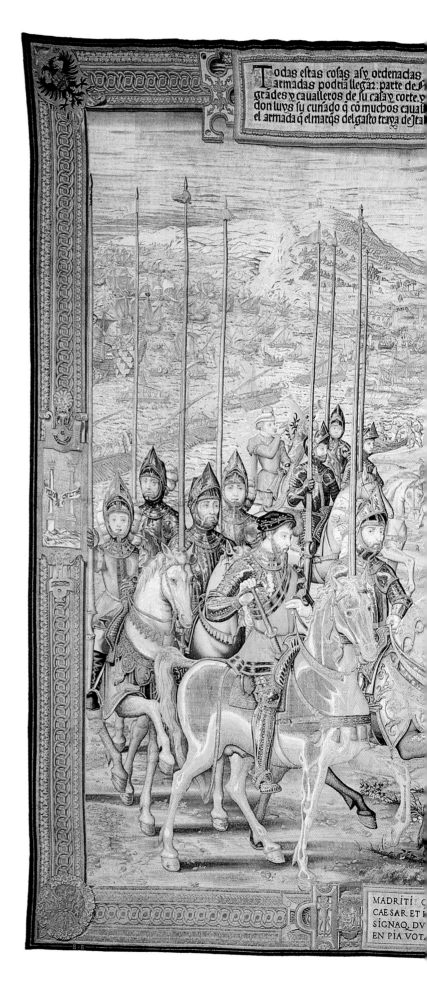

el tiempo cóforme a lo que al Emperador le parecia que conuenia partyr para Barcelona: a la misma sazó que las
ega a Barcelona: donde reconosciendo los aparejos que ally bauia mandado proueer: baze muestra o alarde delos
desunctan las armadas q̃ ally bauiã de venyr, postrero dya de Mayo se bizo a la vela: lleuãdo en su compagnia al Infãte
gueses venya abaliar se en la Jornada. toca é mallorca y méorca y có tiempo algo resyo pasa por el golfo de leó a cerdena dóde balla
represeta é la primera pieça q̃ es la carta de matea y ally de muchas becba vna. de mas de 3 bovelas prosigue el emp̃ su viaje é africa

AC TECTA RELINQVIT AVITA   VT FRETA BINA SECANS BALEARES EXPLICET VNDAS
S BARCINNI CONSTITIT ARVIS.   SARDOASQ. SIMVL: QVO CLASSIS IVSSA COIRE
AT. PROCERES TVRMASQ. RECENSET. GERMANOS ITALAMQ. MANVM VETERESQ. COHORTES
EXPANDENS VELA PER AVRAS   PORTAT IBERORVM ET LIBYCIS ADVERTIT ARENIS.

Charles V, attended by the imperial guard, reviewing his troops before embarking for North Africa (detail of cat. 9, left of center). In the shade of an orange tree on the left sit two men keeping tally of the muster. The city of Barcelona lies in the background.

OPPOSITE: Montserrat, site of a famous sanctuary northwest of Barcelona, rises over 4,000 feet and derives its name (in Latin, *Mons Serratus*) from its serrated ridges (detail of cat. 9, upper right of center).

Monferrate

Knights and a noble mustering for review (detail of cat. 9, far left). In the border is Charles V's personal device—the pillars of Hercules—with his motto, PLUS OULTRE.

the center of the vertical borders. Cartouches in the upper and lower borders contain explanatory inscriptions in Spanish and Latin respectively:

> Todas estas cosas asy ordenadas y medido el tiempo co[n]forme a lo que al Emperador le parecia que convenia partyr para Barcelona: a la misma sazo[n] que las / armadas podria[n] llegar: parte de Madrid y llega a Bar-

celona: donde reconosciendo los aparejos que ally havia mandado proveer: haze muestra o alarde de los / gra[n]des y cavalleros de su casa y corte. y acabadas de junctar las armadas q[ue] ally havia[n] de venyr. postrero dya de Mayo se hizo al la vela: lleva[n]do en su compagnia al Infa[n]te / don luys su cuñado q[ue] co[n] muchos cavalleros portogueses venya a hallarse en la jornada. toca e[n] mallorca y me[n]orca y co[n] tiempo algo rezyo pasa por el golfo de leo[n] a cerdeña do[n]de halla / el armada q[ue] el marq[ue]s del gasto traya de Italia como se represe[n]ta e[n] la primera pieça q[ue] es la carta de marear y assy de muchas hecha una: de mas de. 350 velas prosigue el emp[erad]ᵒʳ su viaje e[n] africa.

(Once all these things have been put in order, and the time calculated for the emperor to depart for Barcelona and for the fleets to arrive, he leaves Madrid and arrives in Barcelona where, after examining the equipment he has ordered to be supplied, he reviews the grandees and knights of his house and court and, having gathered together the fleet that was to assemble there, sets sail on the last day of May, accompanied by the infante Dom Luis, his brother-in-law, who, together with many Portuguese knights, has come to take part in the expedition. Stopping at Mallorca and Menorca, and facing rather rough seas, he passes through the Gulf of Lions to Sardinia, where he finds the fleet the marquis del Vasto has brought from Italy, as is represented in the first piece, which is the navigation chart, and there, making one of many, the emperor continues his voyage toward Africa with more than 350 ships.)

MADRITI CAMPOS AC TECTA RELINQVIT AVITA
CAESAR ET IN LAETIS BARCINNI CONSTITIT ARVIS.
SIGNAQ[VE] DVM LVSTRAT. PROCERES TVRMASQ[VE]
    RECENSET.
EN PIA VOTA FACIT EXPANDENS VELA PER AVRAS

VT FRETA BINA SECANS BALEARES EXPLICET VNDAS
SARDOASQ[VE] SIMVL:QVO CLASSIS IVSSA COIRE
GERMANOS ITALAMQ[VE] MANVM VETERESQ[VE]
    COHORTES
PORTAT IBERORVM ET LIBCIS ADVERTIT ARENIS.

(Caesar leaves the plains and ancestral dwellings of Madrid and takes up a position in the fertile fields of Barcelona. While he parades the standards, he reviews the leaders and the troops. Lo! As he unfurls his sails to the winds, he offers up devout prayers, so that cleaving a path through two channels he may spread out over Balearic and Sardinian waves at the same time: whither the fleet that has been ordered to assemble brings Germans, and the Italian contingent, and veteran Spanish forces, and steers toward the North African shore.)

5. Horn 1989, I, p. 186, points out that Dom Luis (1506–1555) was twenty-nine at the time and suggests that the youth in the center foreground represents the page of the horseman preceding him.

EXHIBITIONS
International Exposition, Barcelona, 1888
International Exposition, Spanish Royal Pavilion, Paris, 1900, no. 6
"Toison d'Or à Bruges," Brussels, 1907
Empress Hall, London, 1914
International Exposition, Barcelona, 1929
"Portugal en España," International Exposition, Lisbon, 1940

LITERATURE
Houdoy 1873; Pinchart 1875, p. 418; Engerth 1889; Madrazo 1889, cuaderno 1, "Tapicería de la conquista de Tunez: La revista de Barcelona," n.p., pl. 1; Valencia de Don Juan 1903, I, pp. 29–53, esp. p. 33, II, pls. 56–65, esp. pl. 57; Calvert 1914; Tormo Monzó and Sánchez Cantón 1919, pp. 95–100, pl. XXXIV; Calvert 1921, pp. ix–x, 32–47, esp. p. 40, pls. 32–43, esp. pls. 33, 34; Göbel 1923, I:1, pp. 311–314, 392–393; Steppe 1968, pp. 748–754; Calberg 1969; Schneebalg-Perelman 1982, pp. 208–209, fig. 133; Junquera de Vega and Herrero Carretero 1986, pp. 73–92, esp. p. 77; Horn 1989.

The device of Burgundy, crossed ragged staves and a firesteel (detail of cat. 9, lower right). In the guard border of the tapestry is the mark of the weaver, Willem de Pannemaker of Brussels.

Children at Play

 A probable antecedent to this series is the *Giochi di putti*, now lost, which was designed by Giovanni da Udine and woven by Pieter van Aelst in 1520 for Pope Leo X. Giulio Romano may have drawn inspiration from that set when he executed the cartoons for *Children at Play*, woven for Cardinal Ercole Gonzaga by Nicholas Karcher in 1540.[1]

When Philip II left the Netherlands in 1559, never to return, he followed his father's advice and directed Antoine Perrenot de Granvelle, the first archbishop of Malines and later cardinal, to remain as counselor to the regent, Margaret, duchess of Parma (1522–1586). For the next five years, a period during which he held the reins of government in Flanders, Granvelle acquired an important collection of tapestries, most of them woven in the workshop of Willem de Pannemaker, purveyor to Charles V and Philip II.

For a set of tapestries that Pannemaker made for the cardinal at a later date, he used as models the cartoons created by Giulio Romano for the Gonzaga family, which had remained in their possession until 1572. This new set was woven during the first six months of 1574.[2]

On the death of the cardinal in 1586, Philip II bought several tapestries at the auction of his estate. Among them was probably a set called "Grapevines and Naked Children," which was listed in the inventories drawn up by the Royal Tapestry Office at the time of the king's death in 1598. Only four pieces of that set survive today.[3]

The games that the putti, children of the nymphs, played in leafy gardens were described by the second-century Greek Sophist Flavius Philostratus in his *Imagines*, which is thought to be the iconographic source of Giulio Romano's compositions.

1. Delmarcel and Brown 1988.
2. Ibid., pp. 109, 115–116.
3. "Tapicería del Rey Felipe II. Cargos contra diferentes personas," March 18, 1621. Archivo de Palacio, Casa, Oficios, legajo 919, pliego 107.

OPPOSITE: Putti disporting themselves among the branches of a vine arbor (detail of cat. 10, upper left)

10 *Vine Arbors and Children Picking Grapes*

Children at Play: fourth tapestry
Workshop of Willem de Pannemaker (active 1535–78),
after a cartoon by Giulio Romano (1499–1546)
Brussels, 1574
Weaver's mark
Gold, silver, silk, and wool
13 ft. 1 in. x 15 ft. 7 in. (400 x 480 cm.)
Madrid, Palacio Real
Inv. PN. S.33/4

The composition of the tapestry is divided into three scenes by two pairs of oak trees, the branches of which are entwined with wild grapevines encircling their trunks and weighing down their crowns with clusters of ripe grapes. The interlaced branches and vines form a natural pergola that serves as the setting for the games of the naked putti disposed in groups on the thick grass, and for those who have climbed the trees and are picking fruit to hand down to their playmates.

The lushness of the landscape increases in the distance, where the scene is closed in by buildings and mountains that create a static backdrop in contrast to the dynamic triptych of games and activities in the foreground.

The central figure of the group in the middle is a putto carrying a large, grape-filled basket on his head. One of his playmates is riding a hobbyhorse; this child's expression registers protest at the heedlessness of the boy urinating from the branches overhead.[4] The gestures directed by those on the ground toward their tree-climbing companions above create intersecting lines of sight superimposed on the enlaced grapevines and oaks.

The small group of two putti at the right of the composition, emphasized by the tall crimson pennant crowned with grape clusters that one is holding, counterbalances the five putti at the left, who are arguing over a small vase in the hands of one of them.

The border that frames the scene includes the heads of fauns and satyrs, with vine leaves, tendrils, and clusters of grapes on a gold background.

4. An image described in Francesco Colonna's *Hypnerotomachia Poliphili* (Venice, 1499). See Delmarcel and Brown 1988, pp. 113–114.

EXHIBITION
Exhibition Commemorating the 4th Centenary of the Founding of the Diocese of Ghent, 1959

LITERATURE
Tormo Monzó and Sánchez Cantón 1919, pp. 107–108; Göbel 1923, I:1, p. 313, I:2, pl. 100; Piquard 1950, pp. 121–125; Ghent 1959, I, nos. 22, 23, II, no. 22; Viale Ferrero 1963, pp. 53–55; Dacos 1980; Junquera de Vega and Herrero Carretero 1986, pp. 236–240, esp. p. 240; Delmarcel and Brown 1988; Forti Grazzini 1989, pp. 474–479.

OPPOSITE: The grape picker and his prize (detail of cat. 10, left)

Poppy (detail of cat. 10, lower right)

Vertumnus and Pomona

Three sets of tapestries in the Spanish royal collection represent the love of Vertumnus, god of the seasons, for Pomona, goddess of fruits and gardens, as narrated in book 14 of Ovid's *Metamorphoses*. They form an exceptionally rich and magnificent group of Brussels tapestries.

Of the three sets inventoried in 1880,[1] two—numbers 16 and 18—had been used to decorate the walls of the banqueting room in the Royal Palace in Madrid on the occasion of the wedding of King Alfonso XII (his second marriage) and Maria Cristina of Austria on November 29, 1879. The tapestries in these sets had been cut down and framed in carved and gilded wood moldings to fit the panels of the banqueting room. Only set number 17 survived intact.

In 1878 Alphonse Wauters noted that the tapestries representing the "Loves of Vertumnus and Pomona" and bearing the mark of Georg Wezeler had been acquired by Charles V in Antwerp before 1546.[2] Consequently, set number 18, in which *Vertumnus as a Reaper* and *Vertumnus as a Haymaker* (PN. S.18/1, 2) bore the supposed mark of the weaver or merchant Wezeler, has been designated the *editio princeps*.

The tapestries of the other two sets, numbers 16 and 17, which were woven by Willem de Pannemaker, were acquired by Philip II.[3] The compositions were based on the same cartoons as those used for the *princeps* set, which have been attributed to Jan Cornelisz Vermeyen with Cornelis Bos and Joos van Noevele,[4] the only significant variation being the border motifs. These motifs, described in the inventories as *entrelazo griego* and *arabescos* ("Grecian interlace" and "arabesques"), had previously figured in other sets woven in Pannemaker's workshop, such as the *Conquest of Tunis* and *Fables from Ovid*.

OPPOSITE: "Often he would come with his temples wreathed with fresh hay"—Vertumnus disguised as a haymaker (detail of cat. 11, left).

The scenes of *Vertumnus and Pomona* are a faithful rendering of Ovid's account, portraying Vertumnus's successive transformations before he overcomes Pomona's amorous indifference and wins her love:

> Oh, how often in the garb of a rough reaper did he bring her a basket of barley-ears! . . . Often he would come with his temples wreathed with fresh hay, and could easily seem to have been turning the new-mown grass. Again he would appear carrying an ox-goad. . . . He would be a leaf-gatherer and vine-pruner with hook in hand; he would come along with a ladder on his shoulder and you would think him about to gather apples. He would be a soldier with a sword, or a fisherman with a rod. . . . He also put on a wig of grey hair . . . and, leaning on a staff, came in the disguise of an old woman. (*Metamorphoses* 14.643–656)[5]

The six tapestries of set number 17—showing the god in turn as a haymaker, a plowman, a pruner, an apple picker, and an old woman, before he finally reveals himself to his beloved—are complemented by Vertumnus's metamorphoses into a reaper, a soldier, and a fisherman, depicted in the other two sets.[6]

A total of twenty-two tapestries has survived; nine were lost in 1734 in a fire at Christmastime that destroyed the old Alcázar de las Austrias. A report written the year after the disaster records the loss of tapestries hung in the Secretariat for the Indies and Navy, among them nine pieces belonging to the "Story of Pomona."[7]

1. "Inventario y registro histórico de las Tapicerías de la Corona existentes en el Real Palacio de Madrid, en el año de 1880": set no. 16, 10 pieces; set no. 17, 6 pieces; set no. 18, 8 pieces. Archivo del Servicio de Conservación del Patrimonio Nacional.
2. Alphonse Wauters, *Les Tapisseries bruxelloises: Essai historique sur les tapisseries de haute- et de basse-lice de Bruxelles* (Brussels, 1878) pp. 85–86.
3. Göbel 1923, I:1, p. 315.
4. Horn 1989, I, pp. 45–46.
5. Translations of Ovid's *Metamorphoses*, by Frank Justus Miller, are from the Loeb Classical Library edition (London, 1916).
6. *Vertumnus as a Reaper*, inv. PN. S.16/1, S.18/1; *as a Soldier*, inv. PN. S.16/4, S.18/6; *as a Fisherman*, inv. PN. S.16/5, S.18/7.
7. "Relación de lo que falta del reconocimiento que se ha hecho en el Oficio de Tapicería," 1735. Archivo de Palacio, Casa, Oficios, legajo 919.

II *Vertumnus as a Haymaker*

Vertumnus and Pomona: first tapestry
Workshop of Willem de Pannemaker (active 1535–78),
after a cartoon attributed to Jan Cornelisz Vermeyen
(1500–1559) with Cornelis Bos and Joos van Noevele
Brussels, ca. 1560
Weaver's mark
Gold, silver, silk, and wool
14 ft. 1 in. x 21 ft. 3 in. (430 x 648 cm.)
Madrid, Palacio Real
Inv. PN. S.17/1

Vertumnus is portrayed beneath a leafy arbor, which
is supported by caryatids that divide the composition
into three contiguous scenes; he is crowned with
grasses and carries a three-pronged pitchfork over his
left shoulder. Facing him, on the other side of the
arbor, Pomona raises her right arm; in her left hand
she holds the pruning hook traditionally associated
with her. Between the two figures, a nymph bends
over to place a basket of fruit on the marble floor. In
the background, beneath a receding series of arches,
Pomona spurns Pan's dance and the tunes he is play-
ing on his syrinx.

In the middle ground, the open pergola offers
glimpses of the orchards that Pomona has nurtured
and that she has enclosed to prevent her suitors from
entering.[8]

> This was her love; this was her chief desire; nor did she
> have any care for Venus; yet, fearing some clownish vio-
> lence, she shut herself up within her orchard and so
> guarded herself against all approach of man. (*Metamor-
> phoses* 14.634–636)

Detail of the border, cat. 11 (upper right)

Pomona rejecting the advances of Pan (detail of cat. 11, center)

OPPOSITE: Detail of Pomona's dress (cat. 11, lower right)

The egg-and-dart and stylized floral border incorporates a female bust in a wreath at each corner and mythological scenes: a medallion illustrating the metamorphosis of Daphne in both the vertical borders and one of Danaë and the shower of gold in the lower border. The same border design, called *arabescos* in the Tapestry Office inventories, was also used to frame the five pieces of the set entitled *Poems* or *Fables from Ovid*,[9] which was woven in the workshop of Willem de Pannemaker and acquired by Charles V from Georg Wezeler.[10]

The cartouche in the upper border bears a faint Latin inscription on a blue background: FOENI SECA E TRVCATO GRAMINE (Mower fresh from cutting hay).

8. In the Middle Ages the enclosed garden, or *jardin clos*, of the Song of Solomon (4:12) was taken as an image of Mary's virginity; see Guy de Tervarent, *Attributs et symboles dans l'art profane, 1450–1600: Dictionnaire d'un langage perdu* (Geneva: E. Droz, 1958) I, cols. 223–224.
9. Inv. PN. S.19/1–5.
10. Göbel 1923, I:1, p. 311.

LITERATURE
Valencia de Don Juan 1903, I, p. 61, II, pls. 69–74, esp. pl. 70; Tormo Monzó and Sánchez Cantón 1919, pp. 89–92; Calvert 1921, pp. 58–59, pls. 83, 85; Göbel 1923, I:1, pp. 315, 333; Crick-Kuntziger 1927; Henkel 1927, pp. 58–144; Crick-Kuntziger 1929; Niño Mas and Junquera de Vega 1956, pp. 32–33; Kerkhove 1969–72; Kerkhove 1973, pp. 243–251; Steppe 1981b; Schneebalg-Perelman 1982, pp. 212–213, figs. 134, 135; Junquera de Vega and Herrero Carretero 1986, pp. 116–122, esp. p. 117; Horn 1989, I, pp. 43–46.

Basket of fruit at the entrance to Pomona's enclave; and in the border of the tapestry, a medallion depicting Danaë and the shower of gold (detail of cat. 11, center foreground)

Renaissance Arms and Armor from the Patrimonio Nacional

JOSÉ A. GODOY

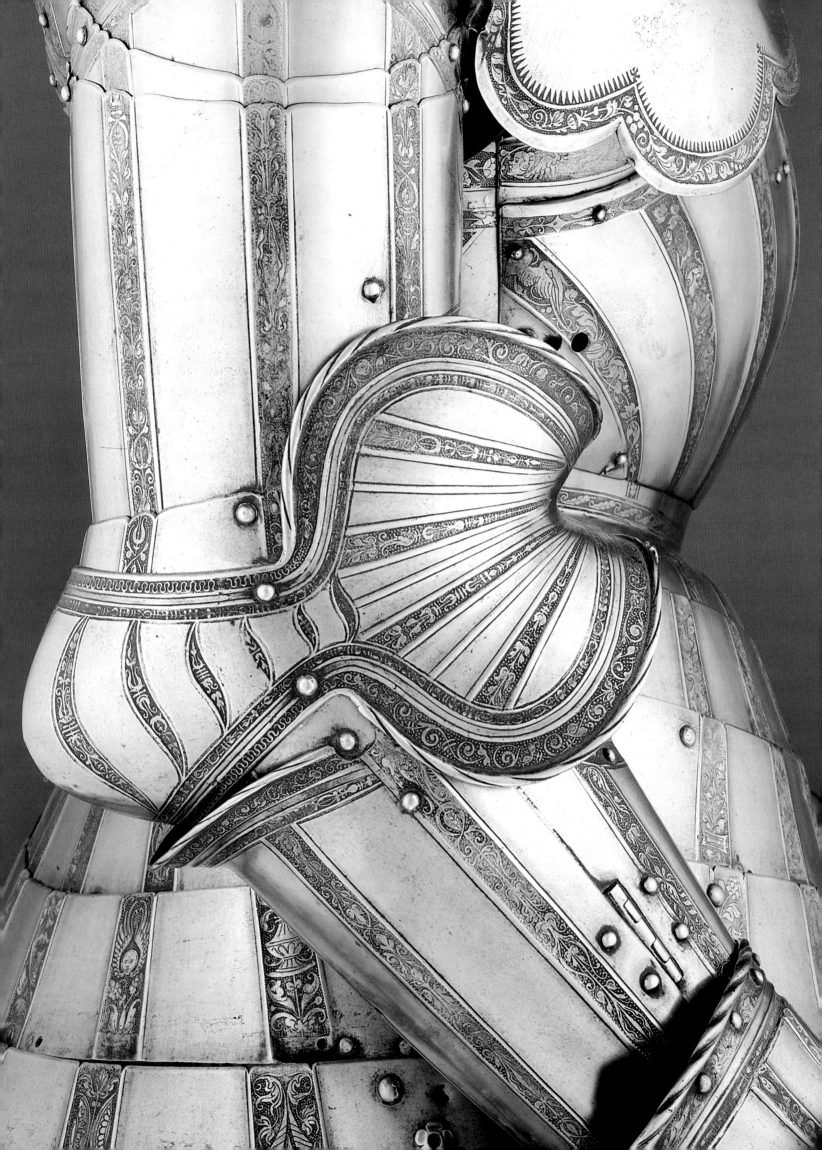

The Royal Armory

The Real Armería of Madrid traces its origins to Philip II's desire to retain the personal armory of his father, Emperor Charles V. That armory had an emotional appeal for him. It also embodied a facet of his father's personality that he must have profoundly admired, one he did not himself possess—that of the army commander who loved to be with his troops. Philip II, a bureaucrat rather than a soldier, did not concern himself, as he might have done, with creating a royal armory systematically bringing together the arms and armor of his immediate forebears and close members of the royal family. Such was not his intention. At the same time he was not wholly insensitive to the issue of historical continuity. Thus, upon the death of his son Don Carlos in 1568, he acquired various arms for the Royal Armory at the auction of the prince's effects, including the sword said to have belonged to Ferdinand the Catholic (cat. 13). In 1582, four years after the death of his half-brother, Don John of Austria, he had the latter's trophies of the battle of Lepanto incorporated into the Royal Armory. He showed no interest, however, in much of the contents of those two "family" armories, which were bought up by nobles and private collectors and dispersed forever. Yet, even if Philip II had no intention of creating an ancestral armory, he succeeded in doing so indirectly through his father's collection, which contained a number of weapons that had belonged to Ferdinand and Isabella, Maximilian I, and Philip the Handsome.

Philip II had the foresight to provide for the future of this fabulous collection of arms, which he personally enriched by adding to it his own armory. In fact,

OPPOSITE: Charles V's tonlet armor from the right, showing the vambrace and couter (detail of cat. 21)

he implicitly made the Royal Armory an entity inalienable from the Spanish crown by his will of March 7, 1594. The same privilege was not extended to the rest of his effects; at his death the precious stones, jewels, tapestries, and other valuable objects were to be placed at the disposition of his executors to enable them to pay his debts and honor his legacies. However, in the event that his son, the future Philip III, wished to retain any of these effects, he was to have the benefit of a modest price to be set by the executors. Three years later, in a codicil of August 23, 1597, Philip II, who by then had fewer financial problems, made more favorable arrangements for the disposition of the tapestry collection, which this time was left to his son outright. In clause 10 of the same codicil, Philip II was careful to specify clearly the extent of the Armory, declaring that it should be considered with everything that it then comprised, just as it was installed in Madrid ("con todo lo que en ella se hallare, de la misma manera que esta puesto en su sala en Madrid"), including all the horse trappings and saddles.

Philip II's wishes were subsequently respected by his son and grandson, Philip III and Philip IV, and later, following tradition, by successive sovereigns. In turn they enriched the Royal Armory, depositing their own arms and sometimes those of a close relative, as in the case of Philip IV's cousin Emmanuel Philibert of Savoy in 1625 and his brother Ferdinand of Austria, known as the Cardinal Infante, in 1643. They also contributed arms given or acquired—for example, those that came from the sale in 1609 of the effects of Alonso Ramírez de Prado and in 1616 from the armorer Andrés de Loydi.

In spite of changes in weaponry, fashion, taste, and cultural interests, the Royal Armory of Madrid has from the outset always been greatly indebted, both qualitatively and quantitatively, to Charles V's armory. It undoubtedly constitutes the very core of the Madrid collection. Philip II deserves credit for having taken adequate measures to prevent the dispersal of his father's collection and his own. His foresight, however, was no mere chance but the result of painful experience following Charles V's death, a fact that has been overlooked in the historiography of the Royal Armory. The dispositions made by the emperor provided that on his death his entire estate should be sold at auction, in order to cover all his debts, obligations, and bequests. Charles died in September 1558 and in February 1559 the executors, in need of money, asked Philip II, who was then in Brussels, for permission to start their work with the effects held in Yuste, Simancas, Valladolid, and Madrid, for many of these objects were suffering damage with time and were also losing value day by day. Philip II requested that they wait until his return to Spain; unfortunately, once in Valladolid he was overwhelmed with work and was unable to deal with the matter before his departure for Aranjuez. There Philip, who was in a difficult financial situation, decided to reserve for himself first of all the whole of his father's armory and communicated to the executors "que queria tomar para si la dha armería y que se entregase a ortega y se tasase" (that he wished to take possession of the said armory and that it should be delivered to Ortega and appraised).

The appraisal could not be made immediately, for the departure of the court from Valladolid had left that city without the necessary experts. However, in view of the fact that certain pieces had originally cost a great deal of money and little return was then expected from it, Philip II was able to acquire the armory of Charles V at a fixed sum of 12,000 ducats. Despite the advantageous price, he was unable to pay cash and had to commit himself to do so within a reasonable time.

The armory was located in Valladolid, in the houses of Francisco de los Cobos, *comendador mayor* of León and secretary to the emperor. This property was situated beside the Colegio de San Gregorio, where another portion of Charles V's effects was held. The nature of those possessions is known, thanks to their appraisal, and it is also known that a town crier was engaged to announce over a two-day period the sale of the effects kept at the Colegio—silverware, tapestries, linens and mattresses, furs, furniture, and garments. Among Charles V's holdings in the castle of Simancas, about six miles from Valladolid, were

swords appraised by Marcos de la Calçada, an otherwise unrecorded swordmaker.

In the emperor's lifetime, the last man responsible for his armory was Peti Joan Brunc, "His Majesty's armorer." Upon the latter's death, his wife, María Escolastras, as executrix rendered a report on the armory to Juan de Ortega, and a new inventory of its contents was drawn up. This is probably the famous *Relación de Valladolid*,[1] today an incomplete manuscript. It is also very likely that this inventory was reused and that it corresponds with the "Account of the armory entrusted to Ortega," one of the reports and inventories of Charles V's effects that were forwarded in February 1559 to Philip II in Brussels. Succeeding Peti Joan, Juan de Ortega was instructed to maintain and clean the arms at an annual salary of 100 ducats, which was paid until the end of 1563 by Charles V's executors. Philip II kept Ortega in that post until August 1564, when he put the armory into the hands of Antonio Prieto, his "master armorer." In 1565 Philip combined his father's armory and his own on the main floor of a building recently constructed by Gaspar de Vega for the Royal Stables in Madrid. The building, opposite the old Alcázar, existed until the fire at the Royal Armory in 1884.

Although the armor was saved, the fire destroyed the entire museum installation begun in 1881 by Juan Bautista Crooke y Navarrot (1829–1904), count of Valencia de Don Juan. Following the disaster, Alfonso XII (1857–1885) had a new building for the Royal Armory erected next to the old one, which was completed in 1893. Valencia de Don Juan's work of restoring and reorganizing the collection concluded with the publication in 1898 of his *Catálogo histórico-descriptivo de la Real Armería de Madrid*, a volume considered exemplary in its time.

Thanks to the quality and wealth of its historic holdings, the Royal Armory—still housed in its nineteenth-century building adjacent to the Royal Palace—is honored today as part of the national heritage of Spain and one of the world's greatest collections of arms and armor.

1. Archivo General de Simancas, Casa Real, Descargos del Emperador Carlos V, legajo 13, documento 16, Inventario de la Armería de Valladolid. The manuscript can be dated to 1558.

12 *Ceremonial Sword of Ferdinand and Isabella*

Spain, late 15th century
Steel, gold, brass, wood, and cloth
Length overall: 52⅞ in. (134.2 cm.)
Madrid, Real Armería
Inv. G 1

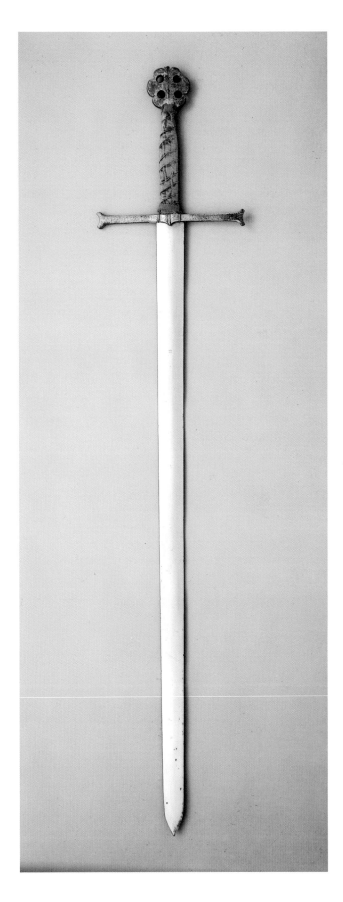

The double-edged blade, of flattened elliptical section, has a brass-inlaid mark on each side in the form
of a circle inscribed in a square, the sides prolonged.
Both cross-guard (quillons) and pommel are gilded.
The quillons are straight, of rectangular section, with
the angles blunted and ends cusped; the quillon block
is shaped and outlined by three vertical moldings.
The top and bottom sides of the quillons are engraved with foliage; the front and back bear inscriptions—TANTO MONTA MEMENTO MEI and TANTO
MONT O MATER DEI ME. The grip is modern. The flat,
six-lobed pommel is pierced with four circles, a shape
that can be read as a cross with arms joined by arched
finials; at the top is a flattened button through which
the tang is riveted. Etched on one face of the pommel
is a bundle of arrows against a hatched background,
and on the other a yoke supported by a cord, with
foliage.

The badges on the pommel of this ceremonial
sword are those of the Catholic Kings, Ferdinand and
Isabella, the first sovereigns of all Spain: the bundle of
arrows of Isabella I of Castile (1451–1504), and the
yoke tied with a knot (an allusion to the legendary
Gordian knot cut by the sword of Alexander the
Great) of Ferdinand II of Aragon (1452–1516), accompanied by his motto on the quillons *Tanto monta* (It's
all the same). By the end of the eighteenth century,
the origin of the sword had become obscure, and it
was thought, probably because of the Marian inscription (*O Mater Dei, memento mei*—O Mother of
God, remember me), to have been presented to Ferdinand by Pope Innocent VIII. In its time, this sword
was used both for conferring knighthood and for the
solemn entries of the monarchs into a town, when it
was borne in procession with the point held upward.
These two uses are confirmed respectively by the
Relación de Valladolid and the Royal Armory inventory of 1594:

Detail of cat. 12, showing the engraved quillons

OPPOSITE: Detail of cat. 12, showing the hilt and the upper part of the blade, stamped with the maker's mark

Una espada ancha vieja de armar Cavalleros con pomo llano agujerado y cruz dorada. (*Relación de Valladolid*)

(An old, broad sword for dubbing knights, with pierced flat pommel and cross, gilded.)

Otra espada de entradas con Vna bayna de rraso carmesi bordada con las Armas de castilla y aragon. (Inventory of 1594)

(Another sword for entries, with a scabbard of crimson satin embroidered with the arms of Castile and Aragon.)

The sword, with a scabbard embroidered with the arms of Castile and Aragon as well as bundles of arrows, figures in the *Inventario Iluminado* of Charles V.[1] However, the scabbard illustrated differs from the sword's present scabbard (G 2), which has been altered at various times and is no longer entirely original. The mark on the blade occurs again in the collection of the Royal Armory, on a javelin (I 95) and on a two-handed sword (A 12) of Philip the Handsome.

1. The *Inventario Iluminado* is the name usually given to two volumes (with a format of 17 x 12⅜ in., or 43 x 31.5 cm.) preserved in the Royal Armory of Madrid (N 18), which contain watercolor drawings of the arms, armor, costumes, saddles, bards, and banners of Charles V. Because of the consistent style of most of the drawings and because the so-called Mühlberg armor (Royal Armory, A 164–187)—dated 1544—is included, the *Inventario Iluminado*, executed in Charles's lifetime, can be dated between 1544 and the year of his death (1558). The two volumes, both incomplete, are similar and illustrate the same objects. Certain missing pages in each were replaced in 1882 by faithful copies made from the volume in which the original was still intact.

LITERATURE
Abadía 1793, p. 13; Jubinal and Sensi [ca. 1839], Suppl., p. 27, pl. 28; Martínez del Romero 1849, pp. 95–96, no. 1765; Valencia de Don Juan 1898, pp. 185–187, fig. 103.

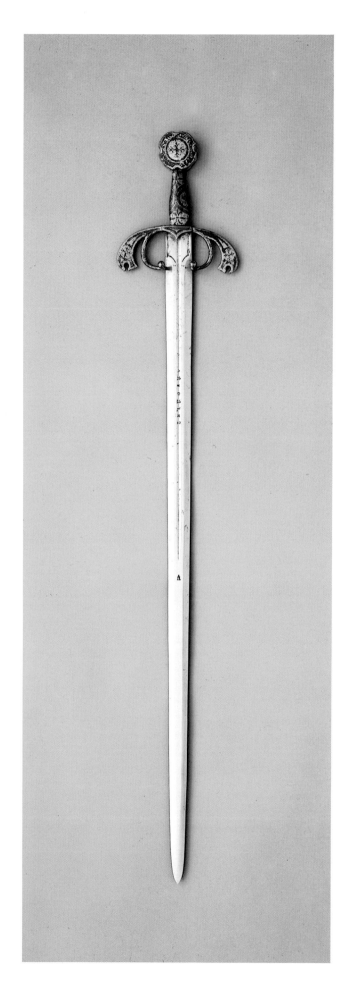

13 *Sword, said to be of Ferdinand II*

Spain, late 15th century
Steel, iron, and gold
Length overall: 37⅞ in. (95.5 cm.)
Madrid, Real Armería
Inv. G 31

The double-edged blade, engraved with lines following the contours of the thickened shoulder (ricasso)
near the hilt, has a longitudinal channel on either
side extending to mid-blade, which accommodates
the two-part signature ANTONIVS/ME FECIT (Antonio
made me) on the obverse and reverse respectively.[1]
The hilt is constructed entirely of iron, engraved,
punched, gilded, and in part blackened. It is ornamented with beaded and dotted bands outlining
the contours and framing medallions that enclose rosettes. The cross-guard (quillons) is flat, curved downward, and flared at the ends, where there is a small
ornamental notch; the arms of the hilt end with short
ball tips projecting at right angles to the plane of the
blade. The grip shows signs of having been short-
ened. The pommel, a disk quartered by notches, is inscribed on the obverse and reverse respectively:
SIEN/PRE GV/ERA/DESEO and PAZ CO/MIGO/NVN/CA VEO
(*Siempre guerra deseo/Paz conmigo nunca veo*—War is
ever my desire/Peace with me I never see). This bellicose legend is not well suited to Ferdinand, who used
the famous motto *Tanto monta.* Nor is there any reason to suppose that it applies to Isabella, his wife,
with whom this sword was associated in the middle
of the nineteenth century, probably because of its
small size. The tradition of Ferdinand's ownership
goes back at least to the middle of the sixteenth century, but always with a "said to be," expressing some
reserve.

Accredited with this royal connotation, the sword
formed part of the armory of Don Carlos (1545–
1568), son of Philip II, and appears in inventories of
the auction of his effects, appraised at five ducats. By
virtue of that tradition, it was placed in the Royal Armory in 1571 by order of Philip II, who was at the
monastery of El Escorial at the time:

Una espada bieja con la guarnicion á la antigua dorada y negra y el puño de yerro dorado que diz que fue del Rey catholico con la bayna de terciopelo negro tassada en cinco ducados que entrego en la armeria de su Magestad por su mandado y con interbencion del prior don antonio su cavallerizo mayor como parece por una cedula de su Magestad su fecha en el monesterio de san lorenço el Real a treinta de jullio de mill quinientos y setenta un años y certificacion del dicho prior del entrego della en la armeria.[2]

(An old sword, gold and black hilt of old-fashioned type, gilded iron grip, said to have belonged to the Catholic King, black velvet scabbard, assessed at five ducats, delivered to His Majesty's armory at his command and with the assistance of the prior Don Antonio, his Master of the Horse, as appears by an order of His Majesty dated at the Monastery of San Lorenzo el Real the thirtieth of July fifteen hundred and seventy-one, and certification by the said prior of delivery thereof to the armory.)

The sword is indeed identifiable in the Royal Armory inventory of 1594, where it is mentioned in similar terms:

Otra espada Corta Española con canal hasta la mitad con una guarnicion de cruz a la Antigua dorada y el puño de hierro dorado que dizen fue del rrey Catolico. (Inventory of 1594)

(Another short Spanish sword, with a channel half the length, with a gilded cross-hilt of old-fashioned type and gilded iron grip, said to have belonged to the Catholic King.)

The sword is today without a scabbard. Evidently, this was refurbished from time to time; the black velvet covering noted in 1571 had by the end of the eighteenth century become red velvet trimmed with gold braid and fitted with a metal chape.

Obverse and reverse of the pommel (detail of cat. 13), inscribed respectively: SIEN/PRE GV/ERA/DESEO and PAZ CO/MIGO/NVN/CA VEO (War is ever my desire/Peace with me I never see)

The Royal Armory formerly had another sword traditionally considered to have belonged to Ferdinand the Catholic, which was presented to the reigning monarch in 1598 by the duchess of Medina-Sidonia. Although the whereabouts of that sword are today unknown, the Royal Armory inventory of 1625 describes it as bearing the names of the three continents of the ancient world, Europe, Africa, and Asia, thus suggesting a date of manufacture prior to the discovery of America in 1492.[3]

In this context, besides the ceremonial sword G 1 in the Royal Armory (cat. 12), mention may be made of a sword of Ferdinand's in the cathedral of Granada, as well as an armor and a helmet of his in Vienna (Hofjagd- und Rüstkammer, inv. A 5, A 645).

1. The maker's mark lower down the blade has been attributed to the Biscotto family, Italian bladesmiths of Villa Basilica, near Lucca (Reid 1965), although no member of the family is known to have worked in Spain. Hispano-Flemish sources, on the other hand, point to the existence of a well-known master

"Antonius" active in Spain—and by implication Spanish—who signed his blades with his Christian name and a mark identical or similar to this one (clearly depicted in a drawing of sword makers' marks, *Senales de las buenas espadas Antiguas*, Madrid, Biblioteca Nacional, MS 10806, fol. 102; L'Hermite [1600] 1896).

2. Archivo General de Simancas, Contaduría mayor de Cuentas, primera época, legajo 1051, fol. 127.

3. "Una Espada corta de A caballo Ancha con una sesma de Recaço dorado con unas letreros que diçen Asia, Africa y Europa con una guarniçion sogueada de una puente dorada Antigua que diçen es de el Rey Don fernando el chatolico quel presento la duquesa de medina sidonia" (A short sword, for use on horseback, with a section of the gilded ricasso with letters reading Asia, Africa, and Europe, with a hilt with roped decoration having a gilt guard of old-fashioned type, said to be that of the king Don Ferdinand the Catholic, which was presented by the duchess of Medina-Sidonia).

LITERATURE

Abadía 1793, p. 6 (A.2, no. 23); Jubinal and Sensi [ca. 1839], I, p. 15, pl. 16; Martínez del Romero 1849, pp. 82–83, no. 1705; L'Hermite [1600] 1896, p. 293; Valencia de Don Juan 1898, pp. 197, 213–214, fig. 127; Gómez-Moreno 1923; Dean 1929, p. 83, no. 76, pl. XXVI; Aguado Bleye 1949; Reid 1965, p. 8; Boccia and Coelho 1975, pp. 339, 348, 355, nos. 124, 184, 248; Thomas and Gamber 1976, pp. 118–120, pls. 52, 53; Norman 1980, p. 80.

14 *Sword, said to be of the Great Captain*

Italy or Spain, ca. 1504–15
Steel, bronze, gold, and cloth
Length overall: 38⅛ in. (96.9 cm.)
Madrid, Real Armería
Inv. G 29

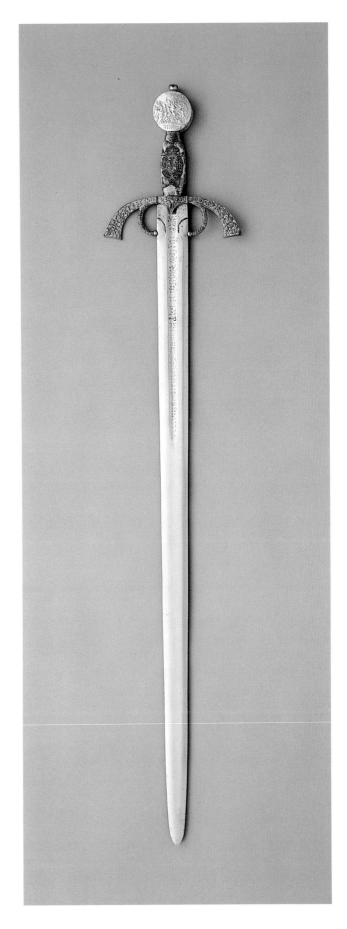

The double-edged blade has a short ricasso and an axial channel extending one-third its length on either side; each channel is etched with a partially effaced Marian inscription—AVE MARIA GRACIA . . . and MATER + GRACIA M . . .—and is stamped about half-way down with the maker's mark, the letter *P*. The guard, comprising quillons and arms of the hilt, is of gilded iron. The flattened quillons expand toward the ends and are arched downward; the arms end with small knobs. The quillons and arms are finely chiseled with foliate scrolls, which also adorn the rim of the circular pommel. The latter is of gilt bronze and measures 2 inches (5.2 cm.) in diameter, with a thickness of ¾ inch (1.9 cm.). Each side is cast with subjects taken from Italian commemorative medals struck in honor of Gonzalo Fernández de Córdoba y Aguilar (1453–1515), who in his own lifetime was known as El Gran Capitán—the Great Captain. On the obverse is a battle scene in the antique style between nude horsemen and foot soldiers before a fortified town; above the scene are inscribed the words CONSALVI/AGIDARI/VICTORIA, and below, DE GALLIS/AD CANNAS (Victory of Gonzalo de Aguilar over the French at Cannae). The reverse bears a shield with the Great Captain's coat of arms supported by Hercules and Janus, the latter with two keys indicating the two entrances to his temple, closed in time of peace and open in time of war. Above and below this composition is an inscription alluding in part to this feature of the cult of Janus: CONSALVVS/AGIDARIVS TVR.[CIS]/GAL.[LIS] DEI R.Q.C.D [REGISQUE CAUSA DEVICTIS]/DICTATOR.III/PARTA ITALI[A]E/PACE IANVM/CLAVSIT (Gonzalo de Aguilar, for God and his king victor over the Turks and the French, commander in chief for the third time, having established peace in Italy closed the temple of Janus).

The sword can be dated to the last decade of Gonzalo de Córdoba's life, about 1504–15. The decoration of the pommel repeats the motifs of the bronze

medals of 1504–05 commemorating the victorious campaign of Apulia (in southeastern Italy) and the celebrated battle of Cerignola in 1503, when Gonzalo defeated the French under the command of Louis d'Armagnac, duke of Nemours. The battle took place near the ancient site of Cannae, where the Carthaginian general Hannibal, who was based in Spain, had defeated the Roman army in 216 B.C. The historical parallel, dear to the classicist spirit of the Renaissance, is evoked by the scene of combat and the inscription proclaiming Gonzalo's victory at Cannae.

There are no conclusive data to confirm or deny the Great Captain's ownership of this sword, nor do we know its provenance or how it came to the Royal Armory. The inscription on the pommel is not in itself a guarantee that Gonzalo owned the sword, even though, typologically, it is a weapon of the period. The use of bronze medals as sword pommels is not unknown, although examples are not very numerous. The scene of ancient combat on the obverse occurs on other medals and as a plaquette, both rectangular and circular in shape; circular plaquettes are double-sided like the one that served as a model for the pommel, but variants are to be found. A sword pommel in the Louvre (inv. Oa 769/Oa 7346) has the same motifs on both sides, but without Gonzalo's name in the inscriptions and with no armorial bearings on the shield. That the Royal Armory's sword G 29 should have been traditionally, and with greater or less conviction, attributed to Gonzalo de Córdoba is understandable, considering the patriotic responses evoked by the reference on the pommel. Nonetheless, in the Royal Armory inventories of 1594 and 1625 the only sword ascribed to the Great Captain is soberly listed alongside the "legendary" swords said to have belonged to Roland, El Cid, and Ferdinand the Catholic:

Otra espada Ancha Española con guarniçion de hierro a lo antiguo con canal hasta la mitad que dizen fue del gran Capitan Con puño de seda negro. (Inventory of 1594)

(Another broad Spanish sword, with iron hilt of old-fashioned type, with channel half the length, said to have been the Great Captain's, with grip of black silk.)

This description, unfortunately too summary to settle the question, might apply equally to this sword

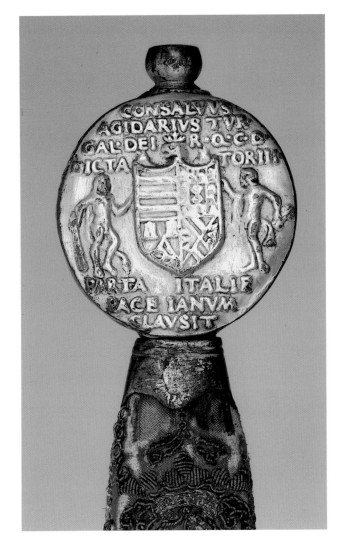

Obverse and reverse of the pommel (detail of cat. 14)

OPPOSITE: Detail of cat. 14, showing the hilt and the upper part of the blade, with its inscription and maker's mark

(G 29) or to another, comparatively plain one (G 30) in the Royal Armory, both of them weapons attributed to the Great Captain in late-eighteenth-century inventories, and even to other swords of the period now or formerly in the Royal Armory. It must be said, however, that G 29, a parade sword of great beauty and rarity, is the only recorded example to bear the name and arms of Gonzalo de Córdoba, and there is no reason to abandon its traditional association.

The sword was greatly prized by later generations. The grip was refurbished in the eighteenth century, with the addition of the terminal ferrules and a red satin covering embroidered with the arms of Spain and the inshield of the Bourbons. At that time, and until at least 1833 (Isabella II), the sword was used in ceremonies when the king conferred knighthood and when the oath of loyalty to the Prince of Asturias was taken by the nobility and high dignitaries of the realm at the beginning of each new reign (the Prince of Asturias being the title given by the king to the immediate heir—male or female—to the throne). The privilege of bearing the sword in the latter ceremony was a hereditary one that devolved on the counts of Oropesa.

LITERATURE
Abadía 1793, p. 8; Jubinal and Sensi [ca. 1839], I, p. 5, pl. 5; Martínez del Romero 1849, pp. 81–82, no. 1702; Molinier 1886, II, pp. 136–140, nos. 634–639; Valencia de Don Juan 1898, pp. 211–212, fig. 125; Nickel 1965, pp. 116, 119–120, 125–126, fig. 10; Pope-Hennessy 1965, p. 31, no. 93, figs. 232, 233; Norman 1980, p. 79; Fulton 1989, p. 154, fig. 21; Lewis 1989, p. 124, fig. 30.

15 Sallet of Philip I

Flanders(?), ca. 1496–1500
Steel and gold
Madrid, Real Armería
Inv. D 14

The sallet has a faceted skull divided into eight sections separated by raised ridges that taper toward the apex, where they meet in a roped or twisted knop. The knop is threaded and fitted with a crest that is screwed in place. The crest (measuring 3⅞ x 3½ in., or 9.8 x 9 cm.) is in the shape of a life-size pomegranate, bursting like a ripe fruit with the seeds showing in relief. The reinforcing plate at the brow has a cusped upper edge ending in tiny palmettes. The pointed tail plate has a lobed upper edge studded with rivets; its lower edge, without ornament, is rolled inward. The pointed visor is pierced with two horizontal openings for sight and, below this, a row of alternating slots and circular holes situated above the horizontal axial line. Below this line the visor steps downward in profile and is pierced only on the right side for ventilation, the left being the side that normally received the blows. The upper edge of the visor, which is removable and secured by hinges, is cusped and palmetted, much like the brow plate. The sallet is stamped twice at the back of the skull, near the nape, with a maker's mark: three crowns aligned vertically.

This helmet has undergone some changes over the centuries. From the *Inventario Iluminado*, we know that a gilt-metal appliqué was riveted around the back of the skull and that another appliqué, which had a lobed border matching that of the bevor, was attached along the lower edge of the tail plate. Both appliqués, as well as the bevor, have been lost. The bevor, which fastened with a strap around the wearer's neck, covered the lower edge of the visor, thus preventing it from opening, and served as protection for the lower face and throat. Originally, the brow reinforce, the tail plate, the ridges of the skull, and the pomegranate were gilded, as were the contour and ridges of the movable visor; only traces of the gilding are preserved today.[1]

Late in the eighteenth century, it was thought that

The sallet complete with its bevor and decorative appliqués (watercolor illustration from the *Inventario Iluminado*)

the sallet had belonged to Boabdil, whose reign as the last Moorish king of Granada ended in 1492. The form of the sallet, however, suggests a Flemish origin that relates it to Philip the Handsome (1478–1506), duke of Burgundy from 1482 and King Philip I of Castile during the last two years of his life. Indeed, the sallet is pictured in the *Inventario Iluminado* of Charles V among the old Flemish arms and armor, and it is also mentioned among the arms of Philip I in the Royal Armory inventory of 1594: "Una zelada con su media vista y una granada dorada en la cresta y una bavera" (A sallet with its half-visor, a gilded pomegranate as crest, and a bevor).

The pomegranate—*granada* in Spanish—as crest must have been intended as a punning reference to Granada, conquered by Ferdinand and Isabella in 1492. This suggests that the sallet was made for, or soon after, the wedding of their daughter, Juana la Loca (Joanna the Mad), to Philip the Handsome in 1496.

1. The pomegranate crest, now of steel, was described at the end of the eighteenth century as silver-gilt (Abadía 1793).

LITERATURE
Abadía 1793, pp. 47–48; Martínez del Romero 1849, p. 16, no. 388; Valencia de Don Juan 1898, pp. 143–144, fig. 83.

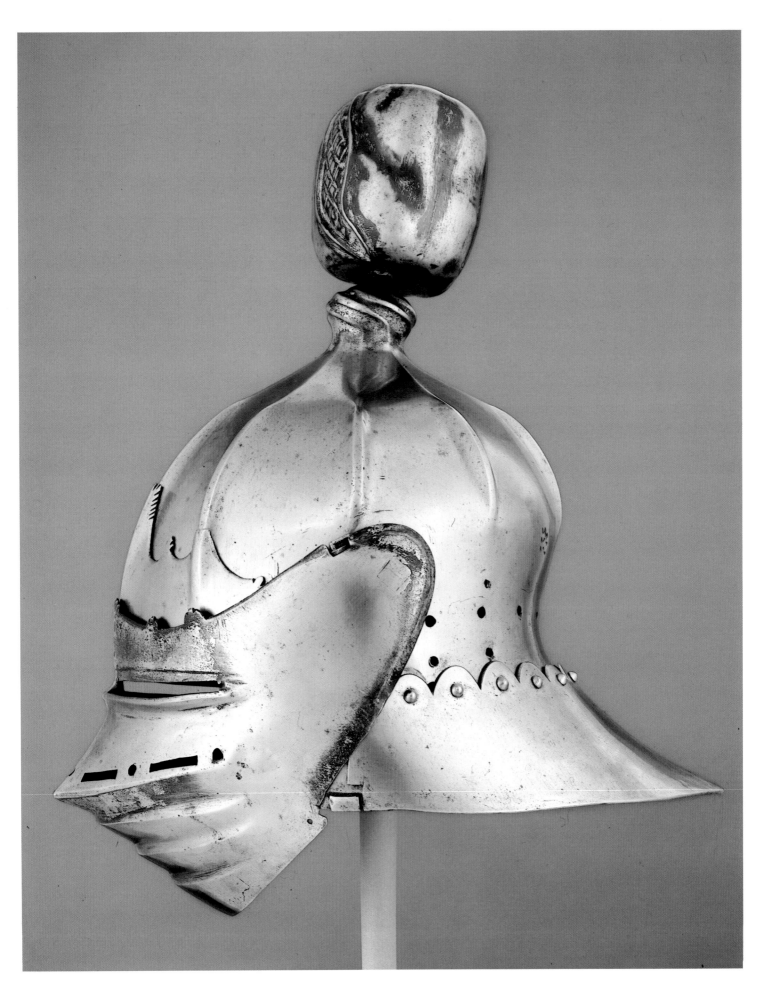

16 *Jousting Armor of Philip I*

Spain (probably Valencia), ca. 1500
Steel, gold, cloth, wood, and leather
Madrid, Real Armería
Inv. A 16

This armor was intended for a form of tournament contest known in Spain as the *justa real*, or royal joust. It is essentially a Spanish variant of the type of armor worn throughout Europe in the fifteenth century for the joust with blunt lances (in German, *Gestech*), in which two contestants on horseback sought to unseat one another or to shatter lances. The armor worn for this joust, of thick plate and thus of considerable weight, consisted of a large helm screwed securely to the cuirass, arms, gauntlets (the left one—the manifer—usually larger, heavier, and of special construction), with a shield (targe) attached at the left side of the chest. Leg armor was usually unnecessary, as the front of the horse was protected by padded cushions in such a way as to safeguard the rider's legs as well.

The massive helm is constructed of three principal plates riveted together, heavily reinforced in the area of the sight. On the right side—blows were received on the left—is a large window for ventilation, opening on hinges and closing with a catch. The base of the helm forms a wide flange that serves to support it on the shoulders; it is cut out in front to fit over the breastplate attachments and is equipped with a hinged iron strap, pierced with four holes through which the helm is fastened to the breastplate. The strap is gilded, as are the brass rivetheads in the shape of rosettes and pinecones that are found at the top of the helm and at the nape. A maker's mark in the form of a fleur-de-lis is struck at the back of the helm at the base.

The torso is protected by a heavy, globose breastplate, covered by a reinforcing plate over the upper chest, and by a half-backplate over the upper part of the back. Below the breastplate are four skirt plates to which is riveted a leather pocket in which to rest the butt of a lance. All the plates are of tinned steel covered with a rich gold brocade that has become worn over time. In the middle of the breastplate is a row of

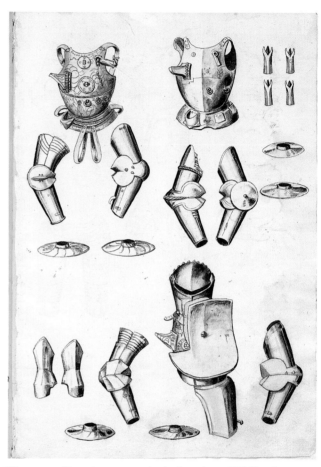

Elements of jousting armor, including that of Philip the Handsome (watercolor illustration from the *Inventario Iluminado*)

four rings for securing weapons; above this are two vertically aligned turning pins by which the reinforcing breastplate is fastened. At the left side of the breast are four staples which pass through corresponding holes in the reinforcing breastplate and over which fits the hinged strap at the front of the helm; a pin descending vertically through the staples locks the helm firmly to the breastplate. The slots in the reinforcing breastplate, through which pass the turning pins on the breast, are framed by gilt-metal washers with decoratively cut and pierced edges. On the right side of the reinforce is a lance-rest consisting of an

Detail of cat. 16, showing the reinforcing breastplate, with its lance-rest, fixtures for attaching the helm, and *flaon* for attaching the targe

iron frame enclosing a triangular block of wood covered with brocade and studded with rivets. On the upper left side hangs a socket (*flaon* in Spanish) with a screw head by which the targe was attached. The inner surfaces of the breastplate and half-backplate are incised with a number of punched lozenges with vertical stripes, suggesting the coat of arms of the city of Valencia.

Detail of cat. 16, showing part of the right side and the faceted couter

Attached at the waist by a strap is a reinforcing plate for the lower left side, to which is riveted a heavy tasset in one piece as protection for the thigh. The armor of the upper limbs is composite and heterogeneous. The shoulders and arms (pauldrons and vambraces) are asymmetrical, the right one having a reinforcing plate at the shoulder and a large faceted elbow plate (couter) that is attached to a smaller, associated couter beneath. The gauntlets are not a pair; the left gauntlet is incomplete, and the right, of mitten construction, is stamped with a mark of Spanish type. Parts of both arms and the tasset are outlined with bands of engraved palmettes and foliated scrolls, stippled and gilded. More elaborate decoration of the same kind covers the entire inner bend of the elbows.

In former times a composite armor that included the helm and cuirass of A 16 was thought to have belonged to Boabdil, the last Moorish king of Granada,

and subsequently to Charles V. Armor A 16, in its present form, was assembled in the late nineteenth century following an illustration in the *Inventario Iluminado*; it was then described as having belonged to Philip I. Although the name of the original owner is not mentioned, the armor is documented, with variations, in the *Relación de Valladolid* and in the 1594 inventory of the Royal Armory as having formed part of the collection of Charles V, and it is indeed very likely to have been made for Charles's father, Philip I:

> Arnes gravado y dorado de real con estas pieças/Un peto cubierto de brocado con rristre dorado/Un flaon y tarjeta/Una sobrebarriga con escarçelon dorado grande/Un aumete blanco todo/Un par de goardabraços con sus braçales digo uno el derecho/Un par de manoplas enteras blancas. (*Relación de Valladolid*)

> (Harness engraved and gilded for the royal joust with these pieces/A breastplate, covered with brocade, with gilded lance-rest/A *flaon* and targe/A stomach plate with large gilded tasset/A helmet, all white/A pair of pauldrons with its vambraces, or rather one, the right/A complete pair of white gauntlets.)

> Otro Arnes de justa rreal con los bordes dorados. Un escarzelon. Un peto y medio espaldar cubierto de brocado su rristre dorado. Un hielmo con su bentanilla liso blanco. Dos guardabrazos yzquierdo y derecho. Dos braçales yzquierdo y derecho. Una sobremanopla. (Inventory of 1594)

> (Another harness for the royal joust with gilded borders. A tasset. A breastplate and half-backplate covered with brocade, its lance-rest gilded. A helm with ventilation hole, polished white. Two pauldrons, left and right. Two vambraces, left and right. One reinforcing gauntlet.)

A second jousting armor in the Royal Armory (A 17), likewise with breastplate and half-backplate covered with gold brocade, bears the same lozenged stamp on the inside of the plates. There, however, the stamp is surmounted by a crown, associating it more closely with the arms of the city of Valencia and serving to confirm the Spanish origin of both armors.

LITERATURE
Jubinal and Sensi [ca. 1839], I, pp. 9–10, pl. 10; Martínez del Romero 1849, p. 40, no. 1004; Valencia de Don Juan 1898, pp. 12–14, pl. 1.

17 *Armor of Philip I*

Flanders, ca. 1500
Steel and gold
Madrid, Real Armería
Inv. A 11

The helmet of this armor is unusual in that it is patterned after an ecclesiastical biretta or a civilian hat of the period; the skull is quartered, with four ridges in relief arranged in a cross, and has two plates riveted to its edges to form a wide, upturned brim. The rest of the armor consists of a bevor of three plates trimmed with mail to protect the lower face and throat; a breastplate of two overlapping plates with articulating lames at the armholes and two skirt plates, the right side of the breast having three staples to receive the lance-rest (now missing); a backplate of two overlapping plates, with two skirt plates; symmetrical defenses for the shoulders and arms (pauldrons and vambraces), with large elbow plates (couters) open at the bend; two faceted roundels (besagews) to protect the armpits; and, lastly, a pair of gauntlets.

All parts are finely etched and gilded at the edges with decorative motifs—scrolled palmettes, foliage, and religious inscriptions in Latin and Old Flemish; the Golden Fleece is shown at the top of the breastplate, and at the top of the lower backplate are two putti supporting a crown. The numerous inscriptions invoke Christ and the Virgin in various standard formulations: for example, IHESVS NASARENUS REX JUDIORUM (Jesus of Nazareth, King of the Jews), along the upper edge of the turnover at the top of the breastplate; and AVE MARIA GRACIA PLENA DOMINVS TECVM BENEDICTA TV BENEDICTA TV [*sic*] IN MVLERIBVS ET (Hail Mary, full of grace, blessed art thou among women and), on the edge of the main plate of the right pauldron. The inscriptions as well as the decorative motifs are set against a hatched background. Except for the skirt plates, the ornamental vocabulary of the backplate is entirely different from that of the other components. Here, in addition to the two putti supporting a crown, we find vases of flowers, grotesque masks, and stylized dragons.

The breastplate, backplate, and both couters are stamped with the maker's mark: an orb and cross sur-

mounted by a crown. The same mark appears on the chanfron A 15[1] and the sallet D 16 of the Royal Armory in Madrid. Other pieces so marked are preserved in Brussels (Musée de la Porte de Hal, II. 40), Cracow (Czartoryski Collection), Glasgow (Scott Collection), London (Wallace Collection, A20), Vienna (Hofjagd- und Rüstkammer, A110) and Windsor Castle (St. George's Chapel).

The resemblance of the steel hat to an ecclesiastical biretta caused the original owner of the armor to be wrongly identified as Cardinal Francisco Jiménez de Cisneros (1436–1517) or Cardinal Infante Ferdinand (1609–1641), Philip IV's brother and governor of the Low Countries. These errors led in turn to confusion over the identity of the maker. In the 1849 catalogue, the mark was said to be that of Jacques Vois, an armorer active a century later than the actual date of this armor, who is known to have made in Brussels an armor for the Cardinal Infante.[2] The mark of the orb and crown, however, is typologically Italian and was very likely that of an Italian armorer working at the court of Philip the Handsome, duke of Burgundy and ruler of the Low Countries. The stamp has recently been attributed to Martin Rondelle, armorer of Bruges and originally of Milan.[3]

The ownership of this armor by Charles V's father is doubly confirmed. First, the illustration in the *Inventario Iluminado* accompanies drawings of other old arms brought from Flanders; second, the same armor is clearly identifiable in the Royal Armory inventory of 1594:

Otro Arnes de seguir, los bordes dorados que fue del Duque philippo. Un peto y un espaldar trançados/Dos Guarda Braços y braçales enteros con sus rrodeletas/ Dos manoplas yzquierda y Derecha/Una caperuza con su bavera.

(Yet another harness, the borders gilded, which belonged to Duke Philip. A breastplate and a backplate,

Detail of cat. 17, showing the etched decoration on the breastplate and the maker's mark

OPPOSITE: Right besagew and couter, the latter stamped with the maker's mark (detail of cat. 17)

each articulated/Two complete pauldrons and vambraces with their besagews/Two gauntlets, left and right/One headpiece with its bevor.)

1. Chanfron A 15 and saddle A 14, traditionally associated with armor A 11, do not in fact belong to it.
2. That armor was recorded in 1643, in an addendum to the Royal Armory inventory of 1625: "Arneses del señor Cardenal ynfante que esta en el cielo. . . . Un cuerpo de harmas de la persona de S.A. con clavazon dorada hecho en bruselas por Jaques Vois" (Harnesses of the Cardinal Infante, who is in Heaven. . . . A body of armor for the person of His Highness with gilded rivets, made in Brussels by Jacques Vois).
3. Norman 1986.

LITERATURE

Jubinal and Sensi [ca. 1839], Suppl., p. 15, pl. 16; Martínez del Romero 1849, pp. 14–15, no. 376; Boeheim 1890, p. 660; Valencia de Don Juan 1898, pp. 8–11, pl. 1; Prelle de la Nieppe 1902, pp. 97–98, no. 40; Macoir 1908, pp. 201–202; Squilbeck 1953, pp. 255–261; London 1960, pp. 7–8, pl. 1; *Connoisseur* 1961; Mann 1962, pp. 7–9; Thomas and Gamber 1976, pp. 179–180; Norman 1986, pp. 1–2 (A20).

18 *Tournament Armor of Charles V*

Attributed to Kolman Helmschmid (1470/71–1532)
Augsburg, ca. 1520
Steel and gold
Madrid, Real Armería
Inv. A 37

The horseman's armor, in part composite, comprises a helm, breastplate, backplate, reinforcing breastplate, lance-rest, asymmetrical shoulder and arm defenses (pauldrons and vambraces), asymmetrical hip defenses (tassets), roundel (besagew) protecting the right armpit, reinforce for the left elbow, right gauntlet (the finger lames covering two fingers at a time), left jousting gauntlet of heavy mitten type (manifer), and complete leg harness of thigh defenses (cuisses), greaves, and toecaps for the mail shoes (sabatons). Associated with this armor is a very handsome concave shield (targe), its field intersected by strips of iron forming lozenge-shaped compartments engraved with the fire-steel of Burgundy; traces of gilding remain.

Despite modifications, some dating to the nineteenth century, the armor as a whole is impressive, with elements of very high technical and artistic quality. The principal plates are outlined with two parallel etched bands separated by a plain one; each etched band features a different foliate motif. One of these, in a more elaborate version, occurs in vertical etched bands that adorn the base of the back of the helm, the backplate, vambraces, and gauntlets. The heavy helm is particularly noteworthy. It weighs 19 pounds 13 ounces (9 kg.) and measures ⅛ inch (3–4 mm.) thick at the edges and ⅜ inch (10 mm.) at the sight, a vulnerable area liable to receive the impact of the adversary's lance; the front half of the helm is smooth for the same reason and has a small window for ventilation on the right side; the rear half, on the other hand, is embossed and etched with two heads of monsters breathing fire. The breastplate is etched at the top with the collar of the Order of the Golden Fleece and is mounted with a lance-rest profusely decorated with plant and figural motifs. Other noteworthy pieces include the half-greaves, their sides delicately etched with a vertical band of foliage, cut out on the back edge along the outline of the leaves; down the

longitudinal median ridge is a band etched with vases of flowers, leaves, and trophies of arms. The composite cuisses and knee defenses (poleyns), although they have the same decoration as the greaves, do not belong to this armor; they appear to have been associated with it only in the nineteenth century and were decorated to match the greaves for exhibition purposes.

The horse armor (bard) is complete and comprises a head defense (chanfron) with ram's-horn earplates and a small shield on the forehead displaying the imperial eagle; neck defense (crinet) and throatpiece of

The bard (watercolor illustration from the *Inventario Iluminado*)

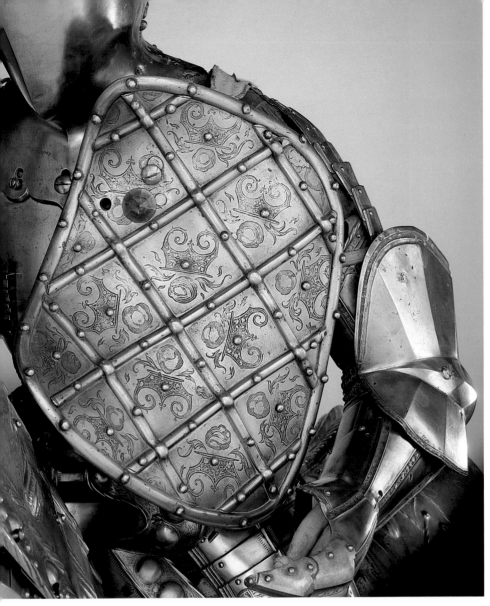

overlapping scales; chest defense (peytral), with a re-movable boss on either side in the shape of a lion's head; flank defenses (flanchards); an enclosed rump defense (crupper) etched with scenes of combat—on the right David and Goliath, on the left Samson and the Philistines; a ram's head as tailpiece; armored reins; and a saddle. The principal pieces are outlined by wide bands of etched or embossed ornament framed by raised roping; the bands are filled with semiglobular bosses or with ribbons wound around a ragged staff hung with decorative tassels. The lower edges of the peytral, flanchards, and crupper are also etched with a frieze of oak leaves. The weight of the bard without the saddle is about 97 pounds (44 kg.).

Both the man's armor and the bard belong to the composite "Valladolid garniture" (A 37–42), so called because of its supposed, though undocumented, use at the festivities held in Valladolid in 1518 when

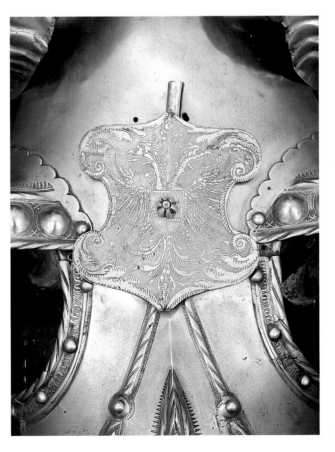

ABOVE, THIS PAGE AND OPPOSITE: Scenes of combat (David and Goliath, Samson and the Philistines) etched on the right and left sides of the crupper (detail of cat. 18)

Charles, king of Spain but not yet elected emperor, was in Spain for the first time. Neither the armor nor the bard bears an armorer's mark, but they are attributable for stylistic reasons to the famous Augsburg armorer Kolman Helmschmid.

Many pieces of this garniture are illustrated in the *Inventario Iluminado*, though scattered over several pages. The bard is shown alone, without the man's armor; displayed on the left side of the crupper is a small shield, now missing, with the imperial eagle. This distinctive bard is readily identifiable in the Royal Armory inventory of 1594:

> Un cavallo De madera Armado con unas bardas blancas gravadas con las Armas del Imperio tiene coplon y silla Arm^da guarneçida de cuero blanco y françaletes y Cuello y testera entera con unos cuernos de carnero y Riendas y petral y lo bajo del cuello de laonas y un penacho en la testera encarnado.

(A wooden horse armed with a white bard engraved with the arms of the empire, with crupper and armored saddle lined in white leather, and flanks and neck and complete chanfron with ram's horns, and reins and peytral and the underside of the neck of plates and a red plume on the chanfron.)

Both armor and bard suffered bomb damage during the Spanish Civil War (1936–39).

LITERATURE
Jubinal and Sensi [ca. 1839], II, pp. 21, 28, pls. 26, 41; Martínez del Romero 1849, pp. 176, 194, nos. 2410, 2517; Valencia de Don Juan 1898, pp. 21–25, pl. v.

Lion's-head boss on the left side of the peytral
(detail of cat. 18)

19 *Armor of Charles V*

Attributed to Kolman Helmschmid (1470/71–1532)
Augsburg, ca. 1525
Steel and gold
Madrid, Real Armería
Inv. A 19

This armor is part of a large and partly heterogeneous garniture—comprising A 19–36 in the Royal Armory—that includes reinforcing or exchange pieces for use in the field or in the tournament. It is generally known as the "*KD* armor" after the initials found on it, or as the armor *de bordes adiamantados* (with diamond-studded borders) in reference to its most obvious decorative feature. Armor A 19 consists of the following elements: a late form of armet, with its characteristic hinged cheekpieces closing at the chin, a pivoted visor, a large, elaborately pierced brow reinforce, and a rondel at the nape; a collar (gorget); a breastplate with a lance-rest and a skirt plate to which two hip defenses (tassets) are attached; a backplate with a skirt plate; asymmetrical shoulder defenses (pauldrons), the right with a circular armpit defense (besagew) and the left with a large upright guard (haute-piece) bearing the initials *KD*; arms (vambraces) open at the bend of the elbows; mitten gauntlets; complete leg harness, comprising thigh defenses (cuisses), greaves, and shoes (sabatons) with attached spurs.

Stylistically, this is one of the finest armors of Charles V, and indeed of his time. The subtle play of plain, smooth surfaces is emphasized by the richly etched and gilded bands that define their contours, framed by borders in relief with rope or scale motifs and studded in places with pyramids or "diamond points." The decorative richness of the armor is enhanced at the pauldrons, besagew, elbows, and tassets by rosettes in relief, radiating channels, and embossed foliage; the last motif appears also on the hinged cheekpieces of the armet, framing the perforations for hearing and ventilation.

Two significant motifs link the armor directly to Emperor Charles V: the collar of the Order of the Golden Fleece, which is etched at the top of the breastplate and backplate; and the conspicuous inter-

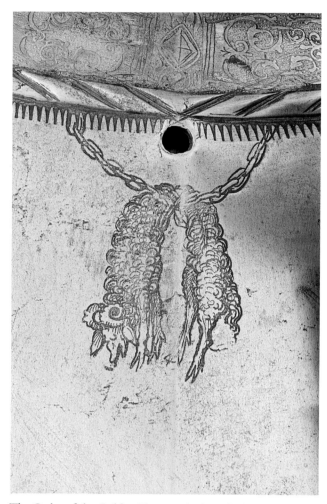

The Order of the Golden Fleece etched on the breastplate

twined initials *KD* spread over the haute-piece of the left pauldron. These initials probably stand for *Karolus Divus* (the Divine Charles) as an imperial title. It may be noted in this connection that in 1549, during the sumptuous festivities given at Binche by Charles's sister Mary of Hungary, regent of the Netherlands, on the occasion of the visit of the emperor and his son the future Philip II, there was a triumphal arch bearing the inscription *Divo Carolo Quinto Caesari Imperatori Maximo*. Likewise, in the 1550 portrait of Charles V in the setting of a triumphal arch

A 19

Armet seen from the right side and the back (details of cat. 19)

engraved by Enea Vico of Parma, the emperor's title begins *Divo Carolo V.*

Armor A 19 has undergone a number of alterations over the years and already appears dispersed over several pages in the *Inventario Iluminado* of Charles V. In the course of time, it even lost its identity, so that by the mid-nineteenth century it was thought to have belonged to Don John of Austria, Charles V's natural son. That fanciful supposition was not an isolated case; it took the place of another, even stranger theory, dating from the late eighteenth century, when the letters *KD* were interpreted as possibly standing for Kalatayud (Calatayud), a town in the Spanish province of Saragossa traditionally renowned for the making of arms.

This armor has long been valued as one of the few "signed" works by the famous Augsburg armorer Kolman Helmschmid, whose mark, together with that of the city of Augsburg, is stamped on the nape of the armet on a small plate riveted to the stem of the skull

below the rondel. The placement of an armorer's mark in this location, at the back of the armor, is highly unusual, as is the fact that the plate on which it is found is not integral with the skull. For if it was Kolman Helmschmid's intention to "sign" his work, it is odd that he should have done so in such an obscure place and on a plate that could easily be lost, and also that he did not mark any of the many other parts of the garniture. The problem of the marked plate, which in my view was added late in the nineteenth century, necessarily casts doubt upon Kolman Helmschmid's presumed authorship of this masterpiece of the armorer's art. On the other hand, from a purely stylistic point of view, it must be said in defense of the attribution that the quality of this armor is fully consistent with that of other armors made by Kolman in the 1520s.

Certain pieces outside the Royal Armory collections feature elements of the etched and gilt decoration found on the "*KD* armor" and originally

The "*KD* armor" from the left, showing the haute-piece with the initials *KD* (detail of cat. 19)

Besagew protecting the right armpit (detail of cat. 19)

belonged to it. The ornament in question consists of a repeated series of eight aligned motifs (nimbed mask, cartouche, winged motif, pair of crossed torches, pair of cornucopias, cross, flower framed by four little circles, and stylized winged female figure). It occurs on a breastplate and backplate in the Museo Nazionale del Bargello in Florence (inv. M 1195), said to have belonged to Ferdinand I (1503–1564), brother of Charles V; and in The Metropolitan Museum of Art, New York, on a pair of vambraces (acc. nos. 29.158.94,95) and a steel toecap for a mail sabaton (acc. no. 42.102.3).[1]

Part of the left gauntlet, tasset, and cuisse (detail of cat. 19)

1. Stuart Pyhrr, personal communication, 1989.

LITERATURE
Jubinal and Sensi [ca. 1839], II, p. 15, pl. 17; Martínez del Romero
1849, pp. 16–18, nos. 383, 402, 421; Boeheim 1891, p. 176, fig. 8;
Valencia de Don Juan 1898, pp. 15–21, pl. II; London 1960, pp. 9–
10, pl. II; Thomas et al. 1974, p. 251, fig. 75 (A 27); Gamber 1975,
pp. 9–10, 21–22, 24–25, 35–37, figs. 15, 16, 55.

20 Horse Armor of Maximilian I

Attributed to Kolman Helmschmid (1470/71–1532)
Augsburg, ca. 1517–18
Steel, gold, and cloth

Horseman's Armor of Charles V

Attributed to Desiderius Helmschmid (1513–1579)
Augsburg, ca. 1540
Steel

Madrid, Real Armería
Inv. A 149

This armor for man and horse was assembled in the late nineteenth century from elements that were originally part of Charles V's armory. Although of different dates, the horse armor (bard) and the horseman's illustrate the superb design and craftsmanship of two generations of Augsburg armorers, Kolman Helmschmid and his son Desiderius, the German armorers Charles V favored above all others.

The bard is one of the most beautiful examples in existence. Dating to about 1517–18, it is thought to have belonged originally to Emperor Maximilian I (1459–1519, reigned from 1508), and to have passed by inheritance in 1521 into the personal armory of his grandson, Charles V.[1] The maker was almost certainly Kolman Helmschmid, who was the finest Augsburg armorer of his time. The designs for the decoration have been attributed to his brother-in-law, the Augsburg painter and graphic artist Hans Burgkmair the Elder (1473–1531), who is known to have decorated armor.

The bard is composed of chanfron, crinet, peytral, and crupper (protecting the horse's head, neck, chest, and hindquarters respectively), as well as armored reins. The chanfron is decorated in relief with large foliated motifs on a dotted background; there was formerly a small escutcheon at the center showing the infant Hercules strangling the serpents sent by Juno, a motif repeated on the front of the peytral (the escutcheon disappeared around 1950). The crinet, of eleven plates, is profusely engraved with motifs, one more fanciful than the other: grotesques, trophies of arms, mythical beasts, bagpipes, peacock, centaur, half-figure of a warrior wearing a sword, fantastic

winged horse, greyhound, jousting helm, jester's head, and stag's head. The outer lateral edges are worked in pierced trefoils, as are the edges of the peytral, crupper, and reins. Except for the chanfron, the front of the peytral, and the tailpiece, which are solid, the rest of the bard is decorated with openwork in low relief, engraved and gilded, set off against a black velvet lining.

The subjects represented on the peytral and crupper, celebrating strength, are arranged symmetrically on either side of the bard. The right side is devoted to the story of Hercules: contending in his cradle with the serpents sent by Juno to kill him, and wrestling with Antaeus (peytral); preparing to strike off the heads of the Lernean hydra, and taming the Cretan bull (the lower and upper registers on the crupper). As biblical pendant to the mythical hero, Samson is represented on the left side: in the arms of Delilah, who is about to cut off his hair, the source of his strength, and bringing down the columns of the house of the Philistines (peytral); breaking the lion's jaw, and carrying off the doors of the gate of Gaza (the lower and upper registers on the crupper).

A magnificent tailpiece, worked in high relief as a dolphin's head, completes the bard.

Like so many armors in the Royal Armory, the bard suffered bomb damage during the Spanish Civil War (1936–39); chiefly affected were the right side of the peytral and crupper, as well as the chanfron, of which the right ear and small napepiece are modern restorations. Other minor restorations include the etched plates covering the crinet strap and a few plates covering the reins. The horse bit is associated.

The infant Hercules strangling the serpents (detail of cat. 20, right side of the peytral)

Samson and Delilah (detail of cat. 20, left side of the peytral)

The armored saddle that originally accompanied this bard was similarly decorated with subjects taken from the lives of Hercules and Samson. Both bard and saddle were illustrated in a volume of pen-and-wash drawings of armor that was formerly in the Thun-Hohenstein Library at Tetschen (Děčín, Czechoslovakia). This volume (Codex a/2), together with another of armor designs (Codex a/8), disappeared at the end of the Second World War. The contents of Codex a/8 are known from photographs; but of Codex a/2 only the page showing this bard and its original saddle is on record.[2]

It was Codex a/8 that illustrated the saddle now mounted with the bard, together with three chanfrons and another armored saddle of Charles V; thus, it too must have belonged to the emperor. The saddle is indisputably a masterpiece and, though unsigned, can like the bard be attributed on stylistic grounds to Kolman Helmschmid. It now consists of five pieces covering the front and rear cantles and is entirely original except for the small plate on the back of the pommel, which is of a different make. The other four plates are ornamented with fanciful figures in relief against a richly etched and gilded backdrop of foliage on a dotted ground. The front cantle has two winged

grotesques on the pommel, one male and one female, back to back; these figures, whose lower bodies form serpentlike tails, are joined by a ring. On each of the side pieces of the front cantle, there is a large mythical figure similar to those described. The rear cantle, made of a single plate, depicts a fight between two marine centaurs, bearded and bareheaded, each with a shield; one is armed with a fork, the other with a trident; between them, in the center of the composition, is an antique vase with flames issuing from it. The saddle, like the bard, suffered damage during the Civil War.

Another of Charles V's saddles in the Royal Armory (A 150), which is stylistically similar to this one, includes in its decoration the imperial eagle and the emperor's personal device—the pillars of Hercules with the motto PLVS VLTER. While the two saddles are roughly contemporaneous, A 149 can perhaps be dated just prior to 1519, the year of Charles V's election as emperor, since it is devoid of any imperial symbolism.

The horseman's armor is composite, having been assembled from elements of several different harnesses that belonged to Charles V. Most of the pieces are datable to the 1530s and can be attributed to Desiderius

Three-quarter view of the bard and the horseman's armor (cat. 20)

Hercules taming the Cretan bull and, below, contending with the Lernean hydra (detail of cat. 20, right side of the crupper)

Hercules and Antaeus (detail of cat. 20, right side of the peytral)

Samson bearing the gate of Gaza and, below, overcoming the lion (detail of cat. 20, left side of the crupper)

Samson bringing down the house of the Philistines (detail of cat. 20, left side of the peytral)

Dolphin's-head tailpiece (detail of cat. 20)

Helmschmid. The armor comprises a close helmet with reinforcing brow plate, collar (gorget), breastplate with left hip defense (tasset), backplate, symmetrical shoulders (pauldrons), arms (vambraces), reinforces for the left pauldron and elbow, left gauntlet for the tilt (manifer), splinted thighs (cuisses), and greaves. The armor lacks gauntlets and shoes (sabatons); the right arm, which is composite and does not match the left, lacks its elbow.

Certain pieces of this armor come from a garniture for use in the field and in the tournament made for Charles V, parts of which, according to the *Relación de Valladolid*, were lost in the ill-fated Algerian campaign against Barbarossa in 1541. A distinguishing feature of the garniture was the image of St. James the

Greater slaying an infidel, which was etched on the two breastplates:

> Un bolante en medio pintado senor Santiago q̄ hera de unas armas q̄ dizen se perdio en la jornada de argel con su sobrebarriga y escarcela. . . .
> Un bolante con media gola que tiene en medio a Senor Santiago. . . . Todo esto es conpanero de un arnes q̄ se perdio en la jornada de argel gravado y dorado. (*Relación de Valladolid*)

(A breastplate, painted in the center with St. James, which belonged to some arms said to have been lost on the expedition to Algiers, with its stomach plate and tasset. . . .
A breastplate with half-throatpiece that has St. James in the center. . . . All this belonged to an engraved and gilt harness that was lost on the expedition to Algiers.)

The second breastplate described, which is represented in the *Inventario Iluminado*, is in fact preserved in the Hermitage Museum, Leningrad, as part of a composite armor (inv. Z.O.3386). The first breastplate, presumably the reinforce for the other, has not been located. It was, however, illustrated with other pieces of Charles V's armor in Codex a/8, one of the volumes of armor designs formerly in the Thun-Hohenstein Library.

The breastplate and backplate now associated with A 149 were selected at the end of the nineteenth century on the basis of the similarity of their decoration to that of the breastplate now in Leningrad, the two breastplates being illustrated side by side in the *Inventario Iluminado*. Both breastplate and backplate are elaborately etched, the principal motifs framed by silhouetted foliage, which is also found on the gorget and reinforce for the left pauldron. In the center of the breastplate, there is a representation of the Virgin and Child surrounded by rays of light, the moon at the Virgin's feet, with two cherubs overhead; and in the center of the backplate is the figure of St. Barbara. Both motifs are frequently found on armors of Charles V.

1. It is not impossible, however, that the bard was made slightly later and for Charles V himself. The horseman shown in an illustration of this bard (Codex a/2, formerly in the Thun-Hohenstein Library at Tetschen, see note 2) has the characteristic aquiline nose of Maximilian I in surviving portraits—for example, the woodcut of 1508 by Hans Burgkmair the Elder.
2. Reproduced in [Leitner] 1888, reg. 4583.

LITERATURE
Gille and Rockstuhl 1835–53, *17e livraison* (17th installment), pl. xcix; Jubinal and Sensi [ca. 1839], II, p. 22, pl. 28; Martínez del Romero 1849, pp. 152–153, no. 2308; [Leitner] 1888, p. iii, reg. 4583; Boeheim 1890, p. 220, fig. 242; Boeheim 1897, p. 24; Valencia de Don Juan 1898, pp. 52–57, pl. x; Reitzenstein 1955, pp. 266–267, figs. 2, 3 (pl. 90); Reitzenstein 1956, p. 94; Reitzenstein 1960, pp. 88, 92; Reitzenstein 1964, fig. 31; Schlegel 1982, pp. 8–10.

Marine centaur wielding a fork (detail of cat. 20, rear cantle of the saddle)

21 *Tonlet Armor of Charles V*

Attributed to Kolman Helmschmid (1470/71–1532)
Augsburg, ca. 1525–30
Steel, gold, and leather
Madrid, Real Armería
Inv. A 93

This armor, with its distinctive tonlet, or skirt, was
used exclusively for the foot tourney in a closed field,
that is, within a fenced enclosure. In such a tournament, pairs of contestants armed "at all points"
fought with swords, the scoring based on the number
and location of hits. The defensive system of the
armor, which is totally enclosed, was devised to leave
the fewest possible weak points accessible to an adversary. As at present assembled, the armor comprises a
close helmet with collar plates, gorget, breastplate,
backplate, symmetrical shoulder defenses (pauldrons)
with upright guards (haute-pieces), reinforces for the
pauldrons, arm defenses (vambraces) closed at the
bend of the elbow, gauntlets, breeches formed of articulated plates (the codpiece is missing), tonlet, thigh
defenses (cuisses) closed at the bend of the knee,
greaves, and mail shoes (sabatons) with steel toecaps.

The armor is part of a garniture of Charles V in
the Royal Armory (A 93–107) called the *Tonelete de
cacerías* (the "Hunt tonlet") because of the animals
featured on the tonlet itself. The armor is ornamented with narrow gilt bands etched with flowers,
foliage, cornucopias, trophies of arms, grotesque
human heads, stylized dolphins, winged creatures,
and so on; these bands run vertically or follow the
contours of the different pieces. The most richly decorated parts are the breastplate and tonlet, where the
width of the etched strips permitted a freer develop-
ment of motifs. The tonlet is in two halves, each of
six plates, closed at the sides. The lowest plate, which
is removable and in two parts, front and back, forms
a border 5⅛ inches (13 cm.) in width. Each half of this
border is gilded and etched with plants on a stippled
ground as a backdrop for four quadrupeds in relief—
formerly gilt, now of bright steel—with bodies
etched to suggest fur and other anatomical details.
These animals include a bear, a stag, and a boar,
pursued by hunting dogs.

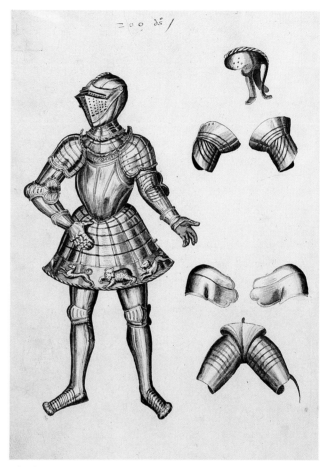

Charles V's tonlet armor, with exchange and reinforcing
pieces (watercolor illustration from the *Inventario Iluminado*)

The garniture, today heterogeneous, has had some
losses and alterations, affecting the tonlet armor only
at certain points. It will be noted, for example, that
the steel toecaps attached to the sabatons are decorated differently from the rest of the armor and do
not belong to it. The breastplate seems to have been
altered, as there are four holes on the upper right side
that have been closed. Their location suggests that
they were made for the attachment of a lance-rest,
which played no part in foot combat.

This armor is illustrated, with some differences, in
the *Inventario Iluminado*. It is also identifiable in

A93

both the *Relación de Valladolid* and the 1594 inventory of the Royal Armory in Madrid:

> Arnes de guerra y para pie con estas pieças ques de tonele dorado y gravado a bandas/Una coroça y espaldar/Una gola/Una celada borgonona/Una escofia/Un par de guardabraços/Unos bracales/Unas grevas enteras con sus quixotes çerrados/Un par de sobacos de laonas blancos/Unas escarçelas/Un batículo/Un tonalete de laonas/Una bregueta/Un par de testeras de cavallo desta labor. (*Relación de Valladolid*)

> (Harness for war and for foot, with these pieces: A tonlet gilded and engraved in bands/A cuirass and backplate/A gorget/A Burgundian sallet/A skull reinforce/A pair of pauldrons/Vambraces/Complete greaves with closed cuisses/A pair of plain armpit plates/Tassets/A culet/A tonlet of plates/A codpiece/A pair of horse chanfrons of the same work.)

> [Arnés] Dorado y Gravado de Alto a Vajo con listas Angostas/Pectto y espaldar sin rristre y un tonelete la orla con una monteria con su gola/Dos Guarda Brazos yzquierdo y derecho con sus bufetas, sus braçales Abiertos/Dos Manoplas sus quixotes enteros con sus navajas/Unas grevas enteras con sus escarpes/Una Zelada borgoñona con la bista rraxada y sus bentanillas/dos Gozetes de laonas que sirven Al dho Tonelete/Una escofia y un barvote/Un morrion con su bentalla/Una sobrecalba/Dos guarda Brazos sin bufetas/Una braga dos pares de escarçelas la una con su bragueta/otros dos Guardabraços rredondos q̄ sirven a este tonelete. (Inventory of 1594)

> ([Harness] Gilded and engraved from head to foot with narrow bands/Breastplate and backplate without lance-rest and a tonlet with a hunting scene on the border, with its gorget/Two pauldrons left and right with their haute-pieces, their vambraces open/Two gauntlets, its complete cuisses with their wings/Complete greaves with their feet/A Burgundian sallet with slit sight and its ventilation holes /Two plate armpit defenses for use with the said tonlet/A skull reinforce and a bevor/A morion with its buffe/A crest/Two pauldrons without haute-pieces/A pair of breeches, two pairs of tassets, one with its codpiece/Another two pauldrons, rounded, for use with this tonlet.)

Although this armor bears no marks, it can be attributed on stylistic grounds to Kolman Helmschmid. It has been identified, despite insufficient documentary evidence, as the armor that Kolman made after traveling from Augsburg to Toledo in

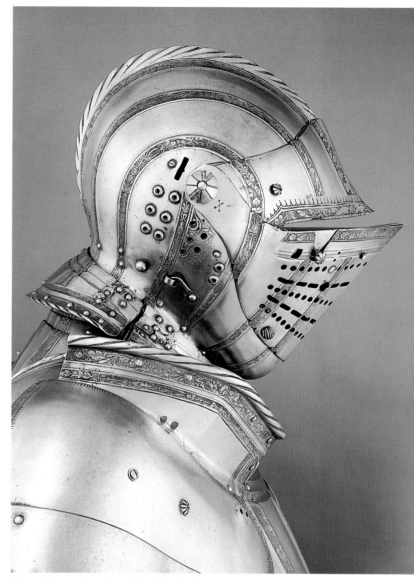

Close helmet from the right (detail of cat. 21)

OPPOSITE: Charles V's tonlet armor from the left (cat. 21)

December 1525 for the express purpose of taking the emperor's measurements.

Two other tonlet armors of Charles V are known. One, which he owned as a child (1512–14), is preserved in Vienna (Hofjagd- und Rüstkammer, inv. A 109). The other is part of a garniture preserved at the Royal Armory in Madrid (A 49), called by virtue of its decoration the *Tonelete de hojas de roble* (the "Oakleaf tonlet").

LITERATURE

Jubinal and Sensi [ca. 1839], Suppl., pp. 31–32, pl. 32; Martínez del Romero 1849, p. 185, no. 2470; Boeheim 1891, p. 195, fig. 12; Valencia de Don Juan 1898, pp. 34–38, pl. VIII.

Hunting dog and wild boar, part of the frieze of animals at the bottom of the tonlet (detail of cat. 21)

Opposite: Etched bands of ornament at the top of the breastplate (detail of cat. 21)

22 Parade Helmet and Shield of Charles V

Filippo Negroli (recorded 1525–51)
Milan, dated 1533
Steel and gold
Diameter: 20¼ in. (51.6 cm.)
Madrid, Real Armería
Inv. D 1, D 2

One of the finest existing specimens of its kind, this parade garniture is the work of the Milanese armorer Filippo Negroli, who with his brother Francesco was the leading master of embossed steel armor *all'antica*—armor in the antique style reflecting Renaissance indebtedness to classical prototypes and motifs.

The skull of the helmet is formed in one piece, embossed and gilded to represent a head of curly hair with a wreath of laurel forming a peak over the brow. There are three collar plates, and the cheekpieces close beneath the chin in two halves of four plates each. The cheekpieces are worked in relief with ears—the lobes pierced for earrings—and sideburns. The lowest rear collar plate is rimmed with a raised dotted braid below a chased strip of foliate scrolls; at the nape two griffins support a medallion bearing the motto PLVS VLTRA and the pillars of Hercules surmounted by the imperial crown. Above this device appear the signature and date: IAC·PHILIPPVS· NEGROLVS·MEDIOLAN·FACIEBAT·M·D·XXX·III (Jacopo Filippo Negroli of Milan made [this] 1533).

The helmet is accompanied by a lower-face defense (buffe) embossed in the same style, with lips, mustaches, beard, and sideburns; the hair is gilded as on the skull. The buffe, which is fastened by a metal strap and buckle, is associated with the helmet but does not match it exactly; the decoration on the front collar plate, instead of continuing the series of motifs from the back, features the collar of the Golden Fleece. The dotted braid along its lower edge is, however, the same, and it appears on the shield as well.

The shield is made of two steel plates riveted together. The center plate is masterfully worked with a lion's head in high relief (approximately 2⁵⁄₁₆ in. [6.5 cm.] high), the encircling mane made up of two superimposed layers of curly locks. Behind this, the second plate, a disk with a hollow center, forms a framework for the lion's head. It has a plain, polished field within a richly decorated border edged on either side by the dotted braid noted on the helmet and bevor. This border is embossed with a frieze of foliate scrolls and griffins, the latter supporting medallions that bear the emblems of Charles V: the pillars of Hercules with the motto PLVS VLTRA; the imperial eagle accompanied by the initials K I (*Karolus Imperator*—Emperor Charles); and the crossed ragged staves and fire-steels of Burgundy, flanked by the same initials. Engraved in the plain field at the top, just below the border, is the signature: IACOBVS·PHILIPPVS· NEGROLVS·MEDIOLANENSIS·FACIEBAT; at the corresponding point at the bottom is the date MDXXXIII. The lion's head, border, and armorer's signature still show remnants of gilding, contrasting with the field of the shield, which was originally darkened.

Both helmet and shield are illustrated in the *Inventario Iluminado*, although not on the same page, and are readily identifiable in the surviving inventories:

Otra çelada morrion con una cabeça redonda a manera de vellocino dorado/Un barbote como una barba dorada. . . . Una rodela el canpo negro y en la mitad una cabeça de leon dorado guarnecida de cuero. (*Relación de Valladolid*)

(Another morion-sallet with rounded skull in the manner of a golden fleece/A buffe like a beard, gilded. . . . A shield, the field black and in the center a lion's head, gilded; lined with leather.)

Una Rodela con Un Rostro de leon dorado/Un Morrion con su crespo dorado, con Un rrostro en el barvote. (Inventory of 1594)

(A shield with a lion's face, gilded/A morion with gilded curls, with his face on the buffe.)

Parade helmet from the right (cat. 22)

Parade shield embossed with a lion's head (cat. 22)

The armorer's signature (detail of cat. 22, top of the shield)

Charles V had another helmet with the skull worked to represent curly hair. This is now in Vienna (Hofjagd- und Rüstkammer, inv. A 498), where it is associated with an armor *all'antica* that was owned by Francesco Maria della Rovere, duke of Urbino (1490–1538). From its decoration, however, the helmet indisputably belongs to the armor of Charles V known as *de las palmas* (the "Palm-branch armor"), parts of which survive in Madrid (Royal Armory, A 114), London (Tower, IV 529), and Worcester, Massachusetts (Higgins Armory Museum, inv. 416). The Vienna helmet is stamped, signed, and dated at the nape: PHILIPPI·NEGROLI·IAC·F/MEDIOLANENSIS·OPUS/ M·D·XXXII. This signature confirms that the "Palm-branch armor," long attributed to Caremolo Modrone, armorer to the duke of Mantua, is in fact the work of Filippo Negroli, made a year earlier than the Royal Armory's parade helmet and shield. A third helmet *all'antica* of this type is in The Metropolitan Museum of Art, New York (acc. no. 04.3.202).

LITERATURE
Jubinal and Sensi [ca. 1839], I, p. 23, pl. 24, II, p. 23, pl. 30, Suppl., p. 27, pl. 27; Martínez del Romero 1849, pp. 39, 156–157, nos. 990, 2316; Valencia de Don Juan 1898, pp. 133–135, pl. XVIII; Grancsay 1921; Thomas and Gamber 1958, pp. 760, 763, figs. pp. 772, 775; Boccia and Coelho 1967, pp. 321–323, 328–330, nos. 249–252, 255; Blair 1974, pp. 22–25; Boccia and Godoy 1985, pp. 92–93, no. 50, fig. 71; Scalini 1987, pp. 13–14, 37, figs. 3, 3 bis, 6; Gamber and Beaufort 1990, pp. 37–38, pls. 10, 11.

23 Parade Shield of Charles V

Filippo Negroli (recorded 1525–51) and Francesco Negroli
(recorded 1542–53)
Milan, dated 1541
Steel, gold, and silver
Diameter: 23¼ in. (59.2 cm.)
Madrid, Real Armería
Inv. D 64

This is one of the most dazzling pieces not only in the Royal Armory of Madrid and in the oeuvre of Filippo and Francesco Negroli, but also in the entire history of Western armor. Form, color, and technique unite in a felicitous synthesis. The superlative gold-and-silver damascening creates an aureole around the Medusa head, which, with its rhythmically waving hair and delicately engraved wings, is modeled with rare mastery.

The shield is made of two concentric plates of steel, the smaller one in the middle riveted to the other, which is hollow at the center. The central plate, 10 inches (25.5 cm.) in diameter and about 2 inches (5 cm.) high, is worked in relief with the winged head of Medusa, her hair spread out in radiating tresses, with a flower above the forehead; two serpents twine around the face, their heads curling inward above, their tails looped together below the chin and tied with a ribbon. Laurel-wreath borders in relief mark the inner and outer edges of the surrounding plate. The field between these borders is divided into three concentric bands, the middle one of which is interrupted, having four plain, raised panels with shaped ends, each containing a recessed lozenge damascened in gold and silver. Cartouches in the lozenges

bear the following inscription: IS TERROR/QVOD VIRTVS/ANIMO ET FOR/TUNA PARET (This object inspires terror, for worth is shown through courage and fortune). The other two bands, and the spaces between the raised panels that link them, are filled with foliate scrolls and bunches of grapes, likewise damascened in gold and silver. On the outer band are four recessed medallions, each supported by winged sirens. Two medallions represent the imperial eagle and two the pillars of Hercules; the eagles' bodies and the pillars, which were of solid gold, are now missing, but their silhouettes and the rest of the engraved and damascened ornament remain.

The inner surface of the shield, at one time lined with black velvet, retains the circular metal strap, attached with eight screws, by which the fabric was secured at the edge. The strap is damascened with two concentric bands of strapwork interlace and foliate scrolls. At the top, facing the bearer, are the signature and date: PHILPP·IACOBI·ET·F·NEGROLI·FACIEBANT· M·D·XXXXI (Filippo Jacopo and F. Negroli made [this] 1541).

Like many other outstanding works owned by Charles V, this piece is described with restraint in the *Relación de Valladolid* and in the inventory of 1594:

The armorers' signature and the date (detail of the back of the shield)

Above and opposite: Parade shield of Charles V, with the head of Medusa (cat. 23)

Una rodela de atauxia canpo negro y en medio un rostro con unas culabras negras y bordes dorados guarnecida de terciopelo negro. (*Relación de Valladolid*)

(A damascened shield, field black and in the center a face with black snakes and gilded borders, lined with black velvet.)

Otra labrada de ataxia con un rrostro Relevado [en]medio. (Inventory of 1594)

(Another damascened item with a raised face in the center.)

Another circular shield with the head of Medusa that probably belonged to Charles V is in Vienna (Hofjagd- und Rüstkammer, inv. A 693a). The embossed decoration of its border appears to allude to one of Charles's African campaigns, probably that of Algiers, suggesting a date around 1541.

LITERATURE
Jubinal and Sensi [ca. 1839], I, pp. 27–28, pl. 27; Martínez del Romero 1849, p. 77, no. 1666; Valencia de Don Juan 1898, p. 154, pl. XXI; Thomas and Gamber 1958, pp. 760, 763, 765–766, fig. p. 781; Gamber and Beaufort 1990, pp. 45–47, pl. 13.

24 Parade Burgonet of Charles V

Filippo Negroli (recorded 1525–51) and Francesco Negroli
(recorded 1542–53)
Milan, dated 1545
Steel and gold
Madrid, Real Armería
Inv. D 30

The burgonet, an open-faced helmet, has a skull made of a single plate of steel embossed with figures in high relief. On the comb is a herm in the shape of a mustachioed Turkish prisoner, his hands behind his back, wearing Roman-type armor and a turban; his lower body forms a fluted column terminating in two spirals below acanthus leaves. At the nape is a grotesque foliate mask. At the front, to right and left respectively, are the winged allegorical figures of Fame and Victory, each holding one end of the Turk's mustache. On the peak over the brow a cartouche damascened in gold bears the inscription: SIC·TVA·/

ĪVICT^E·CAESAR (Thus, through thee, Caesar is undefeated). Under the peak, a separate brow plate bears the armorers' signature and the date in gold: F·ET·FRĀ·DE·NEGROLIS·FACĪ·A·M·D·XXXXV (F[ilippo] and Fra[ncesco] Negroli made [this] in 1545). The cheekpieces are missing.

The burgonet has a browned surface finely damascened in gold in such a way as to emphasize the figures and motifs in relief, while making the inscriptions more legible. The turned edges of the skull and brow plate are richly outlined by a strip of arabesques with a Greek-key border. Wide bands of arabesques

Victory, on the left brow of the burgonet

Captive Turk, on the comb of the burgonet

153

Top of the burgonet (cat. 24), seen from the front

Back of the burgonet (cat. 24)

also occur on either side of the skull below the comb.

This magnificent parade helmet was clearly made, as the inscription shows, for Emperor Charles V. It is the joint work of the brothers Filippo and Francesco Negroli, the presumed creators of a burgonet in the Musée de l'Armée, Paris (inv. H 253), which exhibits a similar iconographic program. A third burgonet with analogous decoration is in the Metropolitan Museum, New York (acc. no. 49.163.3).

LITERATURE

Jubinal and Sensi [ca. 1839], II, p. 23, pl. 29; Martínez del Romero 1849, pp. 159–160, no. 2323; Valencia de Don Juan 1898, pp. 147–148; Dean 1914, pp. 31–32, no. 30, pl. XVI; Thomas and Gamber 1958, pp. 760, 768–769, fig. p. 791; Boccia and Coelho 1967, pp. 323, 333, fig. 273.

25 *Parade Armor of Philip II*

Desiderius Helmschmid (armorer, 1513–1579) and
Jörg Sigman (goldsmith, 1527–1601)
Augsburg, dated 1549–50, 1552
Steel and gold
Madrid, Real Armería
Inv. A 239–242

This parade armor, actually a small garniture with exchange pieces, is one of the finest in the Royal Armory and also one of the high points of the armorer's art. With its minutely detailed decoration in relief, chiseled, engraved, and damascened with gold against the blackened surface, it occupies a unique place in German armor-making, which generally favored etched rather than embossed ornament.

Now incomplete, the armor comprises an open-faced helmet (burgonet), breastplate and backplate of anime construction (articulated transverse lames instead of a single plate), symmetrical shoulder defenses (pauldrons), roundels (besagews, A 239 ter) at the armpits, arm defenses (vambraces), long articulated thigh defenses (cuisses)—detachable to form cuisses of four different lengths—that end with knee pieces (poleyns), codpiece (A 240), and half-greaves; the collar (gorget), gauntlets, and toecaps for the mail shoes (sabatons) are missing. Accompanying the armor are a circular shield (A 241) and five exchange elements: a gorget (A 239 bis) and two small elbow defenses (couters, A 239 ter), to be worn with a mail shirt, and two narrow half-greaves (A 240 bis), to be worn with mail hose. Lastly, a head defense (chanfron, A 239 ter) and saddle (A 242 bis) for the horse complete this magnificent ensemble.

The ornament, despite its richness and profusion, is judiciously controlled, so that the overall effect is one of great elegance. Decorative vertical bands, with others along the contours of the plates, appear on most of the pieces; the bands are separated by plain intervening fields framed with gold damascened festoons and foliate scrolls, which are also used to border the plates and emphasize the transverse articulations of cuirass, pauldrons, and cuisses; the rolled edges of the plates, as well as the comb of the burgonet, are worked in relief to suggest a garland of laurel bound with ribbon. The ornamental vocabulary includes nymphs, satyrs, figures nude or draped in antique style, mythological divinities, the imperial two-headed eagle, winged creatures, masks, garlands, strapwork, and cartouches. Certain important areas, such as the skull of the burgonet, the elbows, and the knees, as well as the shield, are more elaborately decorated with figural and narrative motifs. These include two scenes of combat in the antique style on the burgonet, and on the shield, medallions enclosing the allegorical triumphs of War, Peace, Strength, and Wisdom, with hunting scenes around the edge. Two motifs allude to the owner: the collar of the Golden Fleece on the gorget, breastplate, and couters; and the coat of arms of the crown prince, the future Philip II, on the small shield affixed to the chanfron.

This work, fully signed and dated, is the result of a felicitous collaboration between the celebrated armorer Desiderius Colman Helmschmid of Augsburg and the young goldsmith Jörg Sigman of the same city. The front of the burgonet bears the former's signature and the date: DESIDERIO·COLMAN·IN·AVGVSO 1550, together with the monogram of Jörg Sigman and his initials I S; Sigman's initials are repeated at the nape, with the date 1549. The rear cantle of the saddle is struck with the mark of Augsburg (a pinecone) and that of the armorer (a helm surmounted by a five-pointed star). Finally, the center of the shield is encircled with the inscription: DESIDERIO·COLMAN·CAYS·MAY·HARNASCHMACHER· AVSGEMACHT·IN·AVGVSTA·DEN I5·APRILIS·IM· 1552·IAR (Desiderius Colman, armorer to His Imperial Majesty, completed [this] in Augsburg on the 15th of April in the year 1552).

The presence of so many signatures, apparently unique in the history of armor-making, no doubt reflects the pride of the armorer and the goldsmith in their work. The garniture is the only one of its kind in the oeuvre of Desiderius, who must have seen it as a manifestation of the superiority of his art over that of his famous Milanese competitors, the Negroli. He alludes to this rivalry in one of the hunting scenes in the outer border of the shield—a bull tossing a warrior whose shield is inscribed NEGROL. As for Jörg Sigman, we know from a letter of 1550 addressed to Philip, asking the prince to intercede with the Augsburg authorities in favor of his appointment as master goldsmith, that he had worked on this armor for two years and thought it worthy to cite as evidence of his technical mastery: "por la experiencia de la obra se aclara su scientia" (for the experience gained from the work sharpened his skill).[1]

For his part, Philip surely esteemed this rich and costly armor (its price was apparently 3,000 gold escudos). Formally and stylistically it reflects the restrained and quiet classicism favored by his father, Charles V, who was in Augsburg with his son from July 1550 to May 1551. The emperor must have considered the armor propitious for the leading role Philip undoubtedly played in the festivities and public ceremonies that accompanied the meeting of the Imperial Diet, held to address the delicate matter of the imperial succession.

Philip returned to Spain in July 1551. The shield, which was not finished until April 15, 1552, did not go with him, but the armor he brought from Augsburg originally included some additional pieces no longer to be found in Madrid. Thus, according to the Royal Armory inventory of 1594, this small garniture also comprised a lower-face defense (buffe) to match the burgonet, a second gorget, half-vambraces to be worn with mail sleeves (to which the small existing couters belong), two small pieces for extending the pauldrons, and, of course, the gauntlets and toecaps:

> Una Anima labrada de Relevado y De ataugia que tiene un pecto sin rristre y su espaldar y gola y otra gola de la misma labor que sirve por sí/Dos Guardabraços yzquierdo y derecho rredondos con dos rrodeletas/Dos braçales Abiertos, dos Mandiletes yzquierdo y derecho/Unas escarçelas enteras trançadas con sus Navajas dos peçecuelas para añadir para hazer quixotes/Una bragueta labrada de Ataugia/Unas medias Grevas Redondas/Unas puntas para zapatos de Atauxía/Unas esquinelas de Atauxia/Unos medios braçales labrados de Atauxia con sus navajas que sirven

Right vambrace and couter (detail of cat. 25)

OPPOSITE: Parade armor of Philip II (cat. 25)

> con Mangas de Malla/Otras dos peçecuelas para alargar los guardabrazos/Un Morrion con una bentalla de la misma labor/Una rrodela de la misma labor de las Armas qᵉ tiene quatro carros por guarneçer/Un fuste de una silla con su Armadura de la misma labor de Atauxia/Una testera entera. (Inventory of 1594)

(An anime worked in relief and with damascening, which has a breastplate without lance-rest, and its backplate and gorget, and another gorget of the same workmanship for use by itself/Two rounded pauldrons, left and right, with two besagews/Two open vambraces, two gauntlets, left and right/Complete articulated tassets with their wings, two small pieces to form cuisses/A damascened codpiece/Half-greaves, rounded/Damascened tips for shoes/Damascened greaves/Damascened

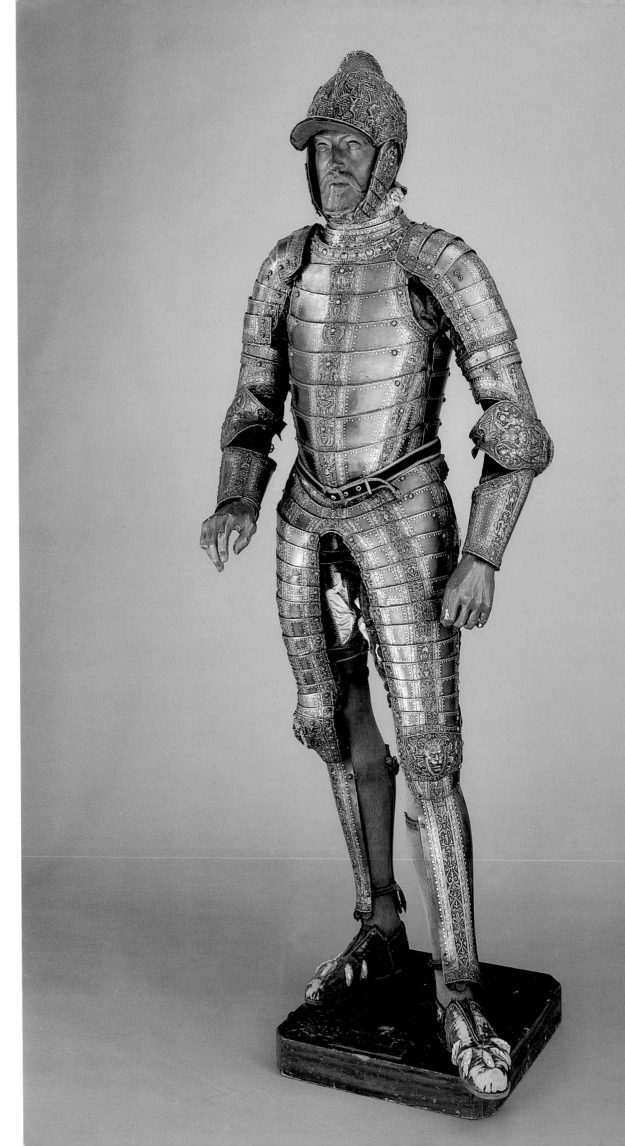

Parade helmet from the right (cat. 25)

OPPOSITE: Gorget and breastplate (detail of cat. 25). The embossed and damascened ornament includes the collar of the Order of the Golden Fleece at the top of the breastplate.

Parade shield (cat. 25)

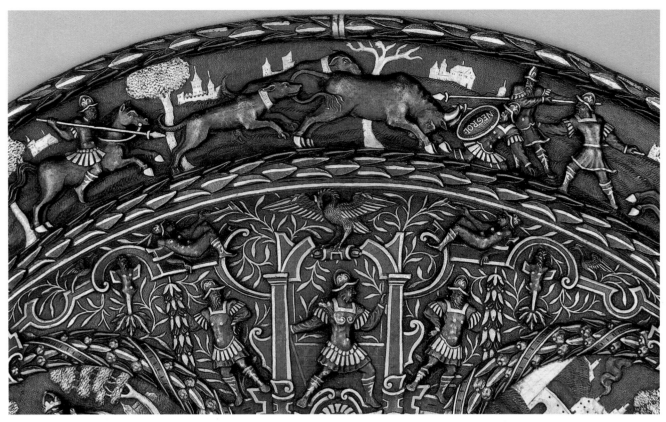

Detail of the shield (cat. 25), with a warrior—his shield inscribed NEGROL—on his knees before a charging bull

Detail of the shield (cat. 25), with the triumph of Peace

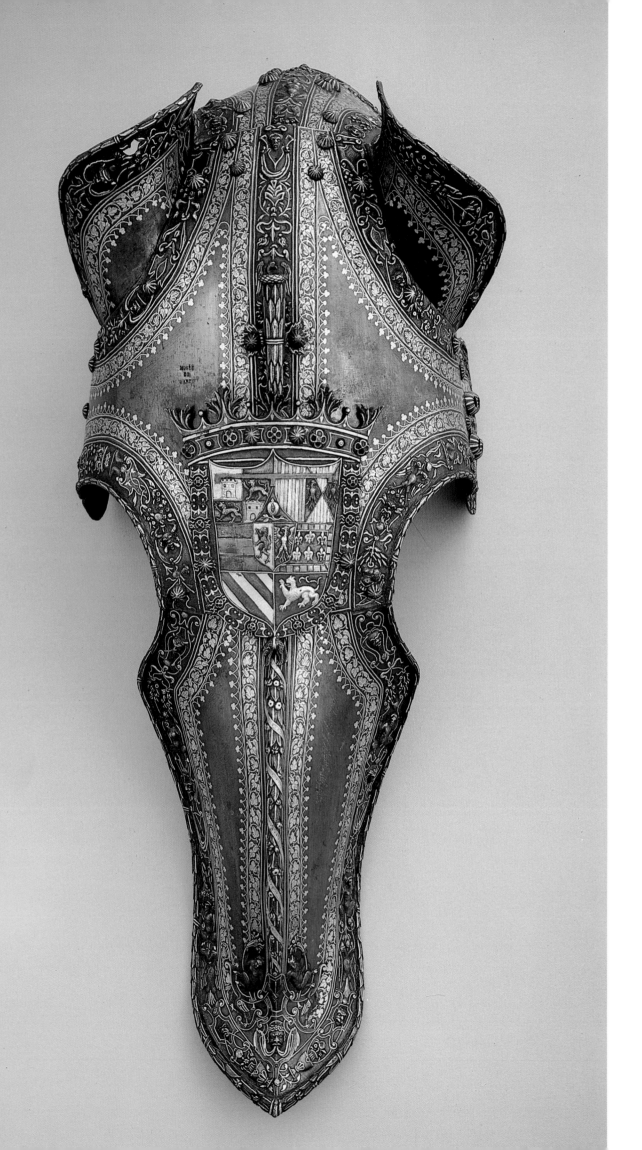

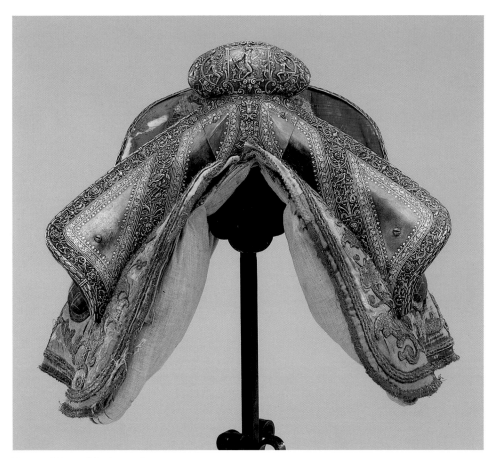

Front of the saddle (cat. 25)

Back of the saddle (cat. 25)

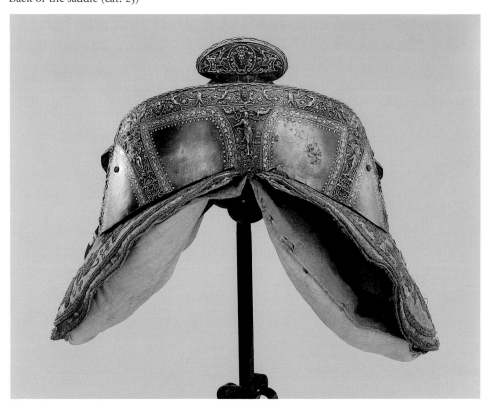

Opposite: Chanfron (cat. 25), with the coat of arms of Philip II before his accession to the throne

Fortune (cat. 25, detail of the back of the saddle, with the maker's mark, left, and the mark of Augsburg, right)

half-vambraces with their wings for use with mail sleeves/Two more small pieces to extend the pauldrons/A morion with a buffe of the same workmanship/A circular shield, which has four chariots, of the same workmanship as the armor, to be fitted out/A saddlebow of armor with the same damascened workmanship/A complete chanfron.)

This small parade garniture lends itself to multiple combinations, exploiting the interchangeability of the defensive pieces for the arms and legs. Such combinations, worn on occasion with either mail garments or civilian dress, allowed the prince, in a politic display of power, to vary at will the military connotations of his royal status. The surviving gorget is the one intended to be worn alone ("for use by itself") over civilian costume; it is decorated with the collar of the Order of the Golden Fleece, which is hidden if mounted below the breastplate; the latter is embossed with the same collar around the neck opening. The shield is without carrying straps and therefore has never been used (still "to be fitted out"). The burgonet had lost its cheekpieces by the middle of the nine-

teenth century; the present ones, finely worked in the style of the armor, are modern and were probably made by the celebrated Spanish metalworker and damascener Placido Zuloaga (1834–1910).

The fate of the parts now missing is unknown. However, they may have been taken from the Royal Armory at the same time as the chanfron, besagews, and detached couters. These five pieces, after having passed through several French collections, eventually entered the Musée de l'Armée in Paris (inv. G.593). In 1914, following a wish expressed by Alfonso XIII of Spain and thanks to a gracious gesture on the part of the French government, they were restored to the Royal Armory in Madrid.

1. Buff 1892.

LITERATURE
Jubinal and Sensi [ca. 1839], II, pp. 23–24, pl. 31; Martínez del Romero 1849, pp. 27, 102, 180–181, nos. 557, 1779, 1780, 2433, 2436; Boeheim 1891, pp. 204–207, figs. 17–24, pls. XIV, XV; Buff 1892, pp. 151–152 n. 6; Valencia de Don Juan 1898, pp. 77–83, pl. XIII; Buttin 1914; Grancsay 1955; Hayward 1956–58; Hayward 1965, nos. II, IIA, IIB; Thomas et al. 1974, p. 256, fig. 103; Thomas 1980, pp. 509–510.

Select Bibliography

TAPESTRIES

Asselberghs 1971
Jean Paul Asselberghs, *Chefs-d'oeuvre de la tapisserie flamande.* Exh. cat., Château de Culan. Bourges: J. Dusser, 1971.

Astier 1907
Colonel d'Astier, *La Belle Tapisserye du Roy (1532–1797) et les tentures de Scipion l'africain.* Paris, 1907.

Beer 1891
Rudolf Beer, ed., "Acten, Regesten und Inventare aus dem Archivo General zu Simancas." *Jahrbuch der Kunsthistorischen Sammlungen des allerhöchsten Kaiserhauses* 12 (1891), part 2: *Quellen zur Geschichte der kaiserlichen Haussamlungen . . . ,* pp. XCI–CCIV.

Calberg 1969
Marguerite Calberg, "Episodes de la Conquête de Tunis: Tapisserie de Bruxelles exécutée en 1565–66 pour le cardinal de Granville." In *De bloeitijd van de Vlaamse tapijtkunst: Internationaal Colloquium (Gent, 23–25 Mei 1961),* pp. 67–98. Brussels: Académie Royale des Sciences, des Lettres et des Beaux-Arts, 1969.

Calvert 1914
Albert F. Calvert, *Spanish Royal Tapestries (The Tunez Series) at the Anglo-Spanish Exhibition.* London, 1914

Calvert 1921
Albert F. Calvert, *The Spanish Royal Tapestries.* London and New York: John Lane, 1921.

Crick-Kuntziger 1927
Marthe Crick-Kuntziger, "L'Auteur des cartons de *Vertumne et Pomone." Oud-Holland* 44 (1927) pp. 159–173.

Crick-Kuntziger 1929
Marthe Crick-Kuntziger, "Tapisserie de l'*Histoire de Vertumne et Pomone." Bulletin des Musées Royaux d'Art et d'Histoire,* ser. 3, 4 (1929) pp. 73–79.

Crick-Kuntziger 1935
Marthe Crick-Kuntziger, "Tapisseries." In *Exposition universelle et internationale de Bruxelles 1935: Cinq siècles d'art.* II. *Dessins et tapisseries,* pp. 47–95. Brussels: Nouvelle Société d'Editions, 1935.

Crick-Kuntziger 1943
Marthe Crick-Kuntziger, "Bernard van Orley et le décor mural en tapisserie." In Société royale d'archéologie de Bruxelles, *Bernard van Orley: 1488–1541,* pp. 71–93. Brussels: Charles Dessart, 1943.

Crick-Kuntziger 1956
Marthe Crick-Kuntziger, "La Tenture de l'Apocalypse." In *Bernard van Orley: Apocalypse,* pp. 32–37. Ars Europeae: Témoignages de la civilisation européenne, I. Antwerp: De Beurs, 1956.

Dacos 1980
Nicole Dacos, "Tommaso Vincidor: Un Elève de Raphaël aux Pays-Bas." In *Relations artistiques entre les Pays-Bas et l'Italie à la Renaissance: Etudes dédiées à Suzanne Sulzberger,* pp. 61–99. Brussels and Rome: Institut historique belge de Rome, 1980.

Delmarcel 1971
Guy Delmarcel, "De structur van de Brusselse tapijtreeks *Los Honores.*" In *Handelingen van het 41ste Congres van de Federatie van de Kringen voor Oudheidkunde en Geschiedenis van België,* II, pp. 352–356. Malines, 1971.

Delmarcel 1977
Guy Delmarcel, "The Dynastic Iconography of the Brussels Tapestries *Los Honores* (1520–1525)." In *España entre el Mediterraneo y el Atlantico: Actas del XXIII Congreso Internacional de Historia del Arte,* II, pp. 250–259. Granada: University of Granada, 1977.

Delmarcel 1979
Guy Delmarcel, "Colecciones del Patrimonio Nacional. Tapices I: *Los Honores.*" *Reales Sitios* 16, no. 62 (1979) pp. 41–48.

Delmarcel 1981
Guy Delmarcel, "De Brusselse wandtapijtreeks *Los Honores* (1520–1525). Een vorstenspiegel voor de jonge keizer Karel V." Ph.D. diss., Catholic University of Louvain, 1981.

Delmarcel and Brown 1988
Guy Delmarcel and Clifford M. Brown, "Les Jeux d'Enfants, tapisseries italiennes et flamandes pour les Gonzague." *RACAR* 15, no. 2 (1988) pp. 109–121, 170–177 (figs. 79–97).

Dollmayr 1901
Hermann Dollmayr, "Giulio Romano und das classische Alterthum." *Jahrbuch der Kunsthistorischen Sammlungen des allerhöchsten Kaiserhauses* 22 (1901), part 1, pp. 178–220.

Duverger 1985
Erik Duverger, "Atelier Bruxellois: Le Globe terrestre." In Jean-Marie Duvosquel and Ignace Vandevivere, eds., *Splendeurs d'Espagne et les villes belges: 1500–1700,* II, pp. 664–666. Exh. cat. Brussels: Palais des Beaux Arts, 1985.

Engerth 1889
Eduard Ritter von Engerth, "Nachtrag zu der Abhandlung über die im kaiserlichen Besitze befindlichen Cartone, darstellend Kaiser Karls V. Kriegszug nach Tunis, von Jan Vermayen." *Jahrbuch der Kunsthistorischen Sammlungen des allerhöchsten Kaiserhauses* 2 (1889) pp. 419–429.

Forti Grazzini 1989
Nello Forti Grazzini, "Arazzi." In *Giulio Romano,* pp. 466–479. Exh. cat., Mantua, Palazzo del Tè and Palazzo Ducale. Milan: Electa, 1989.

Ghent 1959
Museum voor Schone Kunsten. *Vlaamse wandtapijten uit Spanje*. Exh. cat., 2 vols. Ghent, 1959.

Göbel 1923
Heinrich Göbel, *Wandteppiche*: Part I. *Die Niederlande*. 2 vols. Leipzig: Klinkhardt & Biermann, 1923.

Guiffrey 1887
J.-J. Guiffrey, "Destruction des plus belles tentures du mobilier de la Couronne en 1797." *Mémoires de la Société de l'Histoire de Paris et de l'Ile-de-France* 14 (1887) pp. 265–298.

Henkel 1927
M. D. Henkel, "Illustrierte Ausgaben von Ovids Metamorphosen im XV., XVI. und XVII. Jahrhundert." *Vorträge der Bibliothek Warburg* 6 (1926–27) pp. 58–144. Leipzig and Berlin: B. G. Teubner, 1930.

Herrero Carretero 1986
Concha Herrero Carretero, "Tapices donados para el culto de la iglesia vieja." In *Iglesia y monarquía: La liturgia*, pp. 93–99, 129. Exh. cat., IV Centenario del Monasterio de El Escorial. Madrid: Patrimonio Nacional, 1986.

Horn 1989
Hendrik J. Horn, *Jan Cornelisz Vermeyen, Painter of Charles V and His Conquest of Tunis: Paintings, Etchings, Drawings, Cartoons and Tapestries*. 2 vols. Doornspijk: Davaco, 1989.

Houdoy 1873
J. Houdoy, *Tapisseries représentant la Conqueste du royaulme de Thunes par l'empereur Charles-Quint: Histoire et documents inédits*. Lille: L. Danel, 1873.

Junquera 1973a
Paulina Junquera, "La astronomía en los tapices del Patrimonio Nacional." *Reales Sitios* 10, no. 36 (1973) pp. 17–28.

Junquera 1973b
Paulina Junquera, "Tapices de una serie de Escipión en la Real Armería de Madrid." *Reales Sitios* 10, no. 37 (1973) pp. 20–36.

Junquera de Vega and Herrero Carretero 1986
Paulina Junquera de Vega and Concha Herrero Carretero, *Catálogo de tapices del Patrimonio Nacional*: I. *Siglo XVI*. Madrid: Patrimonio Nacional, 1986.

Kerkhove 1969–72
André van den Kerkhove, "Brussels Vertumnus en Pomona-legwerk uit het begin van de XVIIe eeuw." *Gentse bijdragen tot de Kunstgeschiedenis en de Oudheidkunde* 22 (1969–72) pp. 151–181.

Kerkhove 1973
André van den Kerkhove, "Un Essai d'identification, le peintre-cartonnier Joos van Noevele, beau-frère de Willem de Pannemaker." *Bulletin des Musées Royaux d'Art et d'Histoire*, ser. 6, 45 (1973) pp. 243–251.

Madrazo 1880
Pedro de Madrazo [y Kuntz], "Tapicería llamada del Apocalypsi (propiedad de la Corona Real de España). Obra flamenca del siglo XVI." In *Museo Español de Antigüedades*, ed. José Gil Dorregaray, X, pp. 283–419. Madrid: M. Fortanet, 1880.

Madrazo 1889
Pedro de Madrazo [y Kuntz], *España artística y monumental*. Serie IV: *Tapices de la Real Casa; Real Armería de Madrid*, cuadernos 1–3. 6 vols in 1 [text and plates]. Madrid: Viuda de Rodríguez, 1889.

Martin-Méry 1960
Gilberte Martin-Méry, *L'Europe et la découverte du monde*. Exh. cat., Le Mai de Bordeaux. Bordeaux, 1960.

Niño Mas and Junquera de Vega 1956
Felipa Niño Mas and Paulina Junquera de Vega, *Illustrated Guide to the Royal Palace of Madrid*. Madrid: Patrimonio Nacional, 1956.

Paris 1978
Grand Palais. *Jules Romain: L'Histoire de Scipion. Tapisseries et dessins*. Text by Bertrand Jestaz and Roseline Bacou. Exh. cat. Paris: Editions de la Réunion des musées nationaux, 1978.

Pinchart 1875
Alexandre Pinchart, "Les Tapisseries représentant l'histoire de la conquête de Tunis." *L'Art* 3 (1875) pp. 418–422.

Piquard 1950
Maurice Piquard, "Le Cardinal de Granvelle, amateur de tapisseries." *Revue belge d'archéologie et d'histoire de l'art* 19 (1950) pp. 111–126.

Saintenoy 1921
Paul Saintenoy, "Les Tapisseries de la Cour de Bruxelles, sous Charles V." *Annales de la Société Royale d'Archéologie de Bruxelles* 30 (1921) pp. 5–31.

Schneebalg-Perelman 1971
Sophie Schneebalg-Perelman, "Richesses du garde-meuble parisien de François Ier: Inventaires inédits de 1542 et 1551." *Gazette des Beaux-arts*, ser. 6, 78 (1971) pp. 253–304.

Schneebalg-Perelman 1982
Sophie Schneebalg-Perelman, *Les Chasses de Maximilien: Les Enigmes d'un chef-d'oeuvre de la tapisserie*. Brussels: Chabassol, 1982.

Steppe 1968
Jan Karel Steppe, "Vlaams tapijtwerk van de 16e eeuw in Spaans koninklijk bezit." In *Miscellanea Jozef Duverger: Bijdragen tot de kunstgeschiedenis der Nederlanden*, II, pp. 719–765. Ghent: Uitg. Vereniging voor de Geschiedenis der Textielkunsten, 1968.

Steppe 1981a
Jan Karel Steppe, "De reis naar Madrid van Willem de Pannemaker, in augustus–oktober 1561." *Artes Textiles* [Ghent] 10 (1981) pp. 81–124.

Steppe 1981b
Jan Karel Steppe, "Enkeele nieuwe gegevens betreffende tapijtwerk van de Geschiedenis van Vertumnus en Pomona vervaardigd door Willem de Pannemaker voor Filips II van Spanje." *Artes Textiles* [Ghent] 10 (1981) pp. 125–140.

Toledo 1958
Carlos V y su ambiente: Exposición homenaje en el IV centenario de su muerte (1558–1958). Exh. cat., 2nd ed. Toledo, 1958.

Tormo Monzó and Sánchez Cantón 1919
Elías Tormo Monzó and Francisco J. Sánchez Cantón, *Los tapices de la Casa del Rey N.S.: Notas para el catálogo de la colección y de la fábrica*. Madrid: Artes Gráficas Mateu, 1919.

Valencia de Don Juan 1903
Conde Viudo de Valencia de Don Juan, *Tapices de la Corona de España*. 2 vols. Madrid: Hauser y Menet, 1903.

Viale Ferrero 1963
Mercedes Viale Ferrero, *Arazzi italiani del Cinquecento*. 2nd ed. Milan: Antonio Vallardi, 1963.

Wittert 1876
Adrien Wittert, *Les Tapisseries de Liège à Madrid: Notes sur l'Apocalypse d'Albert Dürer ou de Roger van der Weyden*. Liège: J. Gothier, 1876.

ARMS AND ARMOR

Abadía 1793
Ignacio Abadía, *Resumen sacado del inventario general histórico que se hizo en el año de 1793 de los arneses antiguos, armas blancas y de fuego, con otros efectos de la Real Armería*. Madrid: Imprenta Real, 1793.

Aguado Bleye 1949
Pedro Aguado Bleye, "Tanto Monta: La Concordia de Segovia y la Empresa de Fernando el Católico." *Estudios Segovianos* 1 (1949) pp. 381–389.

Blair 1974
Claude Blair, *Arms, Armour and Base-Metalwork: The James A. de Rothschild Collection at Waddesdon Manor*. London: The National Trust, 1974.

Boccia and Coelho 1967
L. G. Boccia and E. T. Coelho, *L'arte dell'armatura in Italia*. Milan: Bramante Editrice, 1967.

Boccia and Coelho 1975
Lionello G. Boccia and Eduardo T. Coelho, *Arme bianche italiane*. Milan: Bramante Editrice, 1975.

Boccia and Godoy 1985
Lionello G. Boccia and José A. Godoy, "Armi europee dal medioevo all'età moderna." In *Museo Poldi Pezzoli*: vol. V. *Armeria*, I, pp. 65–400. Milan: Electa Editrice, 1985.

Boeheim 1890
Wendelin Boeheim, *Handbuch der Waffenkunde: Das Waffenwesen in seiner historischen Entwickelung vom Beginn des Mittelalters bis zum Ende des 18. Jahrhunderts*. Leipzig: E. A. Seemann, 1890.

Boeheim 1891
Wendelin Boeheim, "Augsburger Waffenschmiede, ihre Werke und ihre Beziehungen zum kaiserlichen und zu anderen Höfen." *Jahrbuch der Kunsthistorischen Sammlungen des allerhöchsten Kaiserhauses* 12 (1891) pp. 165–227.

Boeheim 1897
Wendelin Boeheim, *Meister der Waffenschmiedekunst vom XIV. bis ins XVIII. Jahrhundert: Ein Beitrag zur Geschichte der Kunst und des Kunsthandwerks*. Berlin: W. Moeser Hofbuchhandlung, 1897.

Buff 1892
Adolph Buff, "Urkundliche Nachrichten über den Augsburger Goldschmied Jörg Sigman (1548–1601)." *Zeitschrift des historischen Vereins für Schwaben und Neuburg* 19 (1892) pp. 149–180.

Buttin 1914
Charles Buttin, "L'Armure et le chanfrein de Philippe II." *La Revue de l'art ancien et moderne* 35 (1914) pp. 183–198.

Connoisseur 1961
"The Connoisseur's Diary: Church Armour." *Connoisseur* 147 (1961) p. 294.

Cripps-Day 1951
Francis Henry Cripps-Day, ed., *Fragmenta Armamentaria*: II. *Miscellanea*, part 5, *An Inventory of the Armour of Charles V*. N.p.: Butler and Tanner, 1951.

Dean 1914
Bashford Dean, *The Collection of Arms and Armor of Rutherfurd Stuyvesant, 1843–1909*. Allamuchy, N. J.: Privately printed, 1914.

Dean 1929
Bashford Dean, *Catalogue of European Daggers, Including the Ellis, De Dino, Riggs, and Reubell Collections*. New York: The Metropolitan Museum of Art, 1929.

Fulton 1989
Christopher B. Fulton, "The Master IO.F.F. and the Function of Plaquettes." In *Italian Plaquettes*, ed. Alison Luchs, pp. 143–162. Studies in the History of Art, 22. Washington, D.C.: National Gallery of Art, 1989.

Gamber 1975
Ortwin Gamber, "Kolman Helmschmid, Ferdinand I. und das Thun'sche Skizzenbuch." *Jahrbuch der Kunsthistorischen Sammlungen in Wien* 71 (1975) pp. 9–38.

Gamber and Beaufort 1990
Ortwin Gamber and Christian Beaufort, *Katalog der Leibrüstkammer*: II. *Der Zeitraum von 1530–1560*. Vienna: Kunsthistorisches Museum, 1990.

Gille and Rockstuhl 1835–53
F. Gille and A. Rockstuhl, *Musée de Tzarskoe-Selo ou Collection d'armes de sa Majesté l'Empereur de toutes les Russies*. St. Petersburg and Karlsruhe: Velten Editeur, 1835–53.

Godoy 1989
José A. Godoy, "La Real Armería de Madrid." In special 25th anniversary issue of *Reales Sitios* (December 1989) pp. 189–200.

Gómez-Moreno 1923
Manuel Gómez-Moreno, "La espada del Rey Católico." *Coleccionismo* 129 (1923) pp. 89–99.

Grancsay 1921
Stephen V. Grancsay, "Fortuny as a Collector and Restorer of Ancient Arms and Armor." *Bulletin of The Metropolitan Museum of Art* 16 (1921) pp. 235–237.

Grancsay 1955
Stephen V. Grancsay, "A Helmet Made for Philip II of Spain." *Metropolitan Museum of Art Bulletin* n.s. 13 (1955) pp. 272–280.

Hayward 1956–58
J. F. Hayward, "The Sigman Shield." *Journal of the Arms & Armour Society* 2 (1956–58) pp. 21–44.

Hayward 1965
J. F. Hayward, *European Armour.* 2nd ed. Victoria & Albert Museum. London: H.M. Stationery Office, 1965.

Jubinal and Sensi [ca. 1839]
Achille Jubinal and Gaspard Sensi, *La Armería de la Casa Real ou Collection des principales pièces de la galerie d'armes anciennes de Madrid.* Vols. I and II in one; vol. III, Supplement. Paris: Bureau des Anciennes Tapisseries Historiées, n.d. [ca. 1839].

[Leitner] 1888
[Quirin Ritter von Leitner], "Artistisches Quellenmaterial aus der gräfl. Thun-Hohenstein'schen Fideicommiss-Bibliothek in Tetschen." *Jahrbuch der Kunsthistorischen Sammlungen des allerhöchsten Kaiserhauses* 7 (1888), part 2: *Quellen zur Geschichte der kaiserlichen Haussammlungen . . .*, pp. I–VI.

Lewis 1989
Douglas Lewis, "The Plaquettes of 'Moderno' and His Followers." In *Italian Plaquettes*, ed. Alison Luchs, pp. 105–141. Studies in the History of Art, 22. Washington, D.C.: National Gallery of Art, 1989.

L'Hermite [1600] 1896
Jehan L'Hermite, *Le passetemps de J. Lhermite, pub. d'après le manuscrit original.* Vol. II, ed. E. Overleaux and J. Petit. Antwerp: J. E. Buschmann, 1896.

London 1960
Tower of London. *Exhibition of Spanish Royal Armour in H.M. Tower of London.* Text by James Mann. London: H.M. Stationery Office, 1960.

Macoir 1908
Georges Macoir, "Les Armures." In *Les Chefs-d'oeuvre d'art ancien à l'exposition de la Toison d'Or à Bruges en 1907*, pp. 196–216. Brussels: Librairie Nationale d'Art & d'Histoire, 1908.

Mann 1962
James Mann, *Wallace Collection Catalogues: European Arms and Armour.* I. *Armour.* London: Wallace Collection, 1962.

Martínez del Romero 1849
Antonio Martínez del Romero, *Catálogo de la Real Armería.* Madrid: Aguado, 1849.

Molinier 1886
Emile Molinier, *Les Bronzes de la Renaissance: Les Plaquettes.* 2 vols. Paris: J. Rouam and London: Gilbert Wood & Co., 1886.

Nickel 1965
Helmut Nickel, "The Battle of the Crescent." *Metropolitan Museum of Art Bulletin* n.s. 24 (1965) pp. III–127.

Norman 1980
A. V. B. Norman, *The Rapier and Small-Sword, 1460–1820.* London: Arms and Armour Press and New York: Arno Press, 1980.

Norman 1986
A. V. B. Norman, *Wallace Collection Catalogues: European Arms and Armour Supplement.* London: Wallace Collection, 1986.

Pope-Hennessy 1965
John Pope-Hennessy, *Renaissance Bronzes from the Samuel H. Kress Collection: Reliefs, Plaquettes, Statuettes, Utensils and Mortars.* London: Phaidon Press, 1965.

Prelle de la Nieppe 1902
Edgar de Prelle de la Nieppe, *Catalogue des armes et armures du Musée de la Porte de Hal.* Brussels: Musées Royaux des Arts Décoratifs et Industriels, 1902.

Reid 1965
William Reid, "Biscotto me fecit." *Armi antiche* 12 (1965) pp. 3–19.

Reitzenstein 1955
Alexander Freiherr von Reitzenstein, "Die Plattner von Augsburg." In *Augusta 955–1955: Forschungen und Studien zur Kultur- und Wirtschaftsgeschichte Augsburgs*, ed. Hermann Rinn, pp. 265–272. Augsburg: Verlag Hermann Rinn, 1955.

Reitzenstein 1956
Alexander Freiherr von Reitzenstein, "Plattner und Maler." *Die Kunst und das Schöne Heim* 55 (1956) pp. 92–94.

Reitzenstein 1960
Alexander Freiherr von Reitzenstein, "Das Thun'sche Plattnerbuch a/2." *Waffen- und Kostümkunde*, ser. 3, 2 (1960) pp. 88–95.

Reitzenstein 1964
Alexander Freiherr von Reitzenstein, *Der Waffenschmied: Vom Handwerk der Schwertschmiede Plattner und Büchsenmacher.* Munich: Prestel Verlag, 1964.

Scalini 1987
Mario Scalini, *Armature all'eroica dei Negroli.* Florence: Museo Nazionale del Bargello, 1987.

Schlegel 1982
Peter Schlegel, "Die Ross-Harnische Kaiser Maximilians I." *Mitteilungsblatt der Clio- Landesgruppe Stuttgart*, Supplement (April 1982).

Squilbeck 1953
Jean Squilbeck, "Le Travail du métal à Bruxelles." In *Bruxelles au XVme siècle*, pp. 245–271. Brussels: Librairie Encyclopédique, 1953.

Thomas 1980
Bruno Thomas, "Augsburger Harnische und Stangenwaffen (Plattner, Atzmaler, Goldschmiede)" and cat. 897–953. In *Welt im Umbruch: Augsburg zwischen Renaissance und Barock*. II. *Rathaus*, pp. 79–92, 502–537. Exh. cat. Augsburg, 1980.

Thomas and Gamber 1958
Bruno Thomas and Ortwin Gamber, "L'arte milanese dell'armatura." In *Storia di Milano*: XI. *Il declino spagnolo (1630–1706)*, pp. 697–841. Milan: Fondazione Treccani degli Alfieri per la Storia di Milano, 1958.

Thomas and Gamber 1976
Bruno Thomas and Ortwin Gamber, *Katalog der Leibrüstkammer*: I. *Der Zeitraum von 500 bis 1530*. Vienna: Kunsthistorisches Museum, 1976.

Thomas et al. 1974
Bruno Thomas, Ortwin Gamber, and Hans Schedelmann, *Armi e armature europee*. Italian ed. of *Die schönsten Waffen und Rüstungen aus europäischen und amerikanischen Sammlungen*, ed. and trans. Lionello G. Boccia. Milan: Bramante Editrice, 1974.

Valencia de Don Juan 1889; 1890
Conde Viudo de Valencia de Don Juan, ed., "Bilderinventar der Waffen, Rüstungen, Gewänder und Standarten Karl V. in der Armeria Real zu Madrid." *Jahrbuch der Kunsthistorischen Sammlungen des allerhöchsten Kaiserhauses*, part 2: *Quellen zur Geschichte der kaiserlichen Haussammlungen . . .*, 10 (1889) pp. CCCLIII–CCCLIV, pls. 1–23; 11 (1890) pp. CCXLIII–CCLVIII, pls. 24–56.

Valencia de Don Juan 1898
Conde Viudo de Valencia de Don Juan, *Catálogo histórico-descriptivo de la Real Armería de Madrid*. Madrid: Real Casa, 1898.

Index

Page numbers in italic type refer to an illustration. Works catalogued and illustrated are designated by catalogue numbers.